the wise earth speaks to your spirit

the Wise Earth

SPEAKS TO YOUR SPIRIT

52 LESSONS TO FIND YOUR SOUL VOICE

THROUGH JOURNAL WRITING

Janell Moon

Red Wheel
Boston, MA / York Beach, ME

First published in 2002 by
Red Wheel/Weiser, LLC
York Beach, ME
With offices at:
368 Congress Street
Boston, MA 02110
www.redwheelweiser.com

Library of Congress Cataloging-in-Publication Data

Moon, Janell.
   Wise Earth speaks to your spirit / Janell Moon.
      p. cm.
   ISBN 1-59003-014-1 (pbk. : alk.paper)
   1. Spiritual life. 2. Nature—Religious aspects. I. Title.

BL624 .M66235 2002
291.4'32—dc21

                              2001051061

Typeset in Adobe Garamond
Printed in Canada
TCP
09 08 07 06 05 04 03 02
8   7   6   5   4   3   2   1

The paper used in this publication meets the minimum requirements of
the American National Standard for Information Sciences—Permanence
of Paper for Printed Library Materials z39.48-1992 (R1997).

with love
to my son, Greg Szydlowski,
who loves the earth and tiny living things,
and to Wendy, Sherrill, Duey, and Pat.

CONTENTS

ACKNOWLEDGMENTS

These are some of the people of spirit in my life who offered help or who told me stories of times when the wise earth spoke to them.

Joan Annsfire

Kathy Barr

Jeanne Clark

Bob Coates

Maury Cooper

Sherrill Crawford

Pat Cull

Alix Dobkin

Mari-Marks Fleming

C. B. Follett

Emilio Gonzales-Llanes

Barbara Karthman

Luke Kreinberg

Isabelle Maynard

Arlene Melon

Madeline Moore

Doreen Prieter

Sarah Usher

Jerrie Wacholder

Sheila Wells

Katherine Westerhout

Celeste West*

* Celeste West's work appears courtesy of Booklegger Publishing, San Francisco.

INTRODUCTION:
writing about the earth

"Our task is to enter into the dream of Nature
and interpret the symbols."

E. L. GRANT WATSON, *THE MYSTERIES OF THE PHYSICAL LIFE*

MY LIFE'S JOURNEY has been to find connection through a spiritual home. As a child I found writing letters to pen pals and writing stories comforting because I felt connected to something larger than myself. Even now, I remember what it felt like to sit down and write—the humid heat, the slight breeze through the window, the old wooden desk with glass protecting the top, and the feeling of holding time in my hands. I also found similar comfort in nature. Late afternoons in the woods across the street were times of haven. Hours of contentment were given to me in this way! Early on, I discovered that imagination, writing, and nature led me to a place where I belonged.

Later, I started keeping journals and reading voraciously. Through journal writing and reading, I found entries into worlds I hadn't realized were available to me: the heartbeat beneath my feet, the world of mud to reflect how my life might have been formed, the world of all living things that gave both meaning and beauty to my life. I would wake at night and gaze at the moon and its moonbeam. I would slip outside before breakfast to appreciate the ferns and get a peek of the bay. I began to realize that the pink of spring belongs not only to the plum tree but to me. I noticed that the wind that blows the feathers at the back of the mud dabbler egret's neck is the same wind that shifts my hair and cools me. Birds would come to my hanging geranium plants, and I would watch closely as they nested and hatched their babies, all the while thinking of ways I could nurture the child in me. I filled notebooks that explored how I was part of the whole of earth, nature, and all living things. I began to feel the healing powers of the earth come through my body.

I began to see that finding both personal and archetypal meanings is important for our sense of spiritual connectedness. For instance, I have always loved ducks because to me they seem friendly and yet care for themselves. My family says ducks are my favorite animal because they seem so happy on their own; they're so independent. It's true. I love their busy little ways that demand nothing from me. However, since they are seldom alone, they have another archetypal meaning—more of joining or marriage. I can appreciate that meaning too; maybe part of the reason they seem friendly to me is that they stay together in flocks.

My life was made immeasurably richer when I could look at a tree and call it by name: pepper, magnolia, eucalyptus. It was as if I had learned a new friend's name and by calling her by that name I was able to make her more "mine." And to know that the tree is a symbol of the whole of life—the coming together of heaven, earth, and water—made me better notice each tree.

Watching the earth do her seasons then enabled me to step into the seasons of my own life. I could finally feel like the root and the seed and the flowering. By holding the death of the plant in my hands, I became less afraid. I wrote a poem about this process in my life:

Lessons

The earth has a history for you; she can reveal
how to live with scars
holding stories, coastlines carved
through with water and wind
repeating themselves, repeating themselves.
Soon enough she will teach
you that death follows life. Oh I know
you thought you knew but not in your body.
Your body thought you'd always be kissed
by the juice of the berry staining your skin.
Now with further inspection, you see the pink

of the plum tree belongs
to the branch and the root, the flower reappearing
only until the root is done.

Through this process of accepting endings and a deeper spiritual connection with the natural world, something happened in my life that seemed miraculous; my life became one. Finally, everything I did became everything else, and everything I did became part of the whole of my spiritual life. My spiritual learning leaned into every work I touched. The loving of small living creatures, the birds and the squirrels, brought me to a connection with my "earth body."

What I have come to understand is that we use the symbols that are meaningful to us to create a connection to the earth. There are times when I am a "tree person" and need the feel of the bark on my back. Other times I am the wild sea and welcome change in my life. I use the stars in the sky to hold my dreams and wishes.

I like to lie on the earth and feel the power of the living earth beneath me. The Gypsies say, "The earth is our mother, the secret of life comes from the ground." The Apache Indians said all creatures were born from the earth in the beginning, just like a mother births her child. "Tread softly, all the earth is holy ground," says English poet Christina Rossetti. We, too, can begin to feel this holy ground under our feet.

The earth in the psyche represents sensation and stability. It is all that is solid. At times, the earth is represented in our dreams as the elephant or the tortoise, the steady ones. However, I found it interesting to learn that in dream symbolism, earthquakes mean personal disintegration. Earthquakes were also once considered expressions of power either divine or hostile to humanity. They threatened order and therefore had to be appeased so that humanity could have rock and stone and stability.

It was writing in a journal that helped me integrate this new awareness and knowledge. I wrote and asked the earth to help me feel connected. I prayed by writing. I explored in writing the things I noticed on my daily walks. I asked questions of the earth and did research on how rocks have been used in spiritual ceremonies. I found new meaning sitting on large boulders surrounding part of the bay where I lived. I sat there feeling secure and wondering about the need for both stone and the fluid waters. I explored this in writing. Writing about my own connections with the earth helped me go deeper into my feelings and spiritual self, exploring how I had created both solid ground and chaos in my life. I then was able to write what helps me feel emotionally whole and what makes me feel fractured.

The very act of writing has its own connection to the natural world. European pagans used a tree alphabet to send secret messages. Barbara G. Walker, in *The Woman's Dictionary of Symbols and Sacred Objects,* tells of an ancient history where messages were spelled out on a string of leaves. Leaves from different types of trees were each assigned a letter of the alphabet and strung in an order that spelled out a word. The leaf and letter assignment was secret to the group sending the message. Blank leaves not included in the alphabet were used between words. For instance, if you wanted to say, "I come," on a cord, you would string Yew for "I," Willow for a "blank," Hazel for "C," Furze for "O," Vine for "M," White Poplar for "E." This way of communicating was used successfully for many years.

Writing things down slows us down just long enough to consider our emotions, body sensations, and thinking. Clarification helps us live a more spiritual life because we don't have to behave in a knee-jerk reaction. Just to write can give us the pause to take a deeper look into our lives. Journal writing helps us vent, explore, practice, clarify, and even heal feelings. It often helps us act in a way that reflects the spiritual path we have chosen.

What you will find in these pages is a fifty-two-week cycle of essays and related questions about various aspects of the natural world. I wrote the essays to help spark your process of understanding your own connection to the natural world, your own associations with the wild and untamed parts of yourself. You'll find entries on night and sky and parakeets, wind and mud and rain, snakes and tea and thistle. You'll read about the folklore, myth, stories, and symbols connected to each theme. You'll hear about my experiences with the natural world, as well as those of friends, clients, and others. At the end of each essay, you'll find questions. You may want to journal on just one or on all. You may find yourself journaling on what you found in the text or on any ideas that come. It's up to you.

I include a lot of history and myth and folklore because information about the earth from past cultures can help us look at the earth as living and to see it in more imaginative ways. It can help inform our writing. A physicist can tell you that the earth is a mass of atoms, but that doesn't mean it isn't also the ground that the Goddess Mother gave you. Buddhists believe that the rope is the way humans came to earth. Only souls could ascend it to heaven. The Mayan Indians believed there were four pillars of kapok trees at the four corners of the earth to hold it down, and these trees were protected by supernatural guardians. The bottom part of the globe was seen as feminine and the skies masculine. Together they made up the circle of the world.

Through myths we can establish and explore our identity. A myth may present a moral behavior, and we can identify whether we value this behavior or not. The phoenix was so gentle it alighted on nothing and fed on no living thing but dew. This is the same bird that rises to life again from its own ash three days after its death. The appearance of the phoenix signified peace and benevolent rule. We can write what this means to us about authority or what moral lesson is suggested here.

I have tried to call on myths that don't demean women. In this regard, I sometimes use myths as a jumping off place and continue with a story that would better satisfy our souls. Or I might suggest you make up your own story or myth.

We will look at nature in symbolic terms. A symbol can represent some deep, intuitive wisdom that eludes direct expression. We know that this is true when we stumble onto a symbol, perhaps from a dream, that grips us intensely. As we dream of the world burning, we might sense that we have lost our fire while we are living a busy life. We may discover the many meanings fire has for us.

I am reminded that early American peoples recognized dreams as special times of communication between humans and the supernatural world. In dreams, humans can contact companion spirits and enter dialogues with ancestors and gods. Because of this, we'll pay attention to our dream symbols in this book.

Archetypal symbols, or universal images, have always been with us. They can not be explained rationally or explained away by rational arguments. Take, for instance, the dragonfly with its existence documented in fossils back to ancient times, more than 180 million years ago, and its archetypal meaning of immortality and regeneration. With its amazing pigments that reflect light, just like a rainbow, we know it is one of our ancient ancestors, spreading beauty over our ponds and marshlands. We could believe that, just as dragons were strict guardians of the temples, the dragonfly, as it hovers, flies backwards, and speeds along at 30 mph, guards the temple of heaven and allows us passage with just our longing.

We will also look at the meanings ascribed to the elements: earth, fire, water, and air. As Barbara G. Walker writes in *The Woman's Dictionary of Symbols and Sacred Objects,* "The real origin of the elements lay somewhere in the Neolithic Age, when people discovered that there are only four possible ways to dispose of their dead (other than cannibalism): burial, cremation, sinking in waters, or exposure to carrion birds of the air. All four of these funerary practices were known to the ancients, who envisioned death as a reversal of birth, a return to the Mother who brought forth all life in the world." It is through Greek literature that this knowledge was passed into European tradition.

Nature has its clues and gives answers. The American folklore of the horseshoe for luck shows us that we have symbols and ways to be helped by the animal world. We can see a raccoon in the park and begin to write how it feels to see such a pretty fellow. From this feeling we might write about the raccoon as the masked part of ourselves. We can explore how we want to be both revealed and concealed to ourselves and others. We can ask ourselves through journal writing what this is about for us.

We can use our journal writing to muse about what the animals know. For instance, birds know how high or low to build their nests in any given season. If we notice their building habits and the heights of the nests, we can tell when flooding will happen. We can call on this wisdom in our writing.

We can look beyond and beneath traditional rituals for their origins in the earth. "Baptism rituals were originally centered on motherhood and the maternal prerogative of name-giving. Mothers pronounced their infants' names while squirting them with milk from their breasts," writes Barbara G. Walker. She goes on to say, "The Egyptians did a great deal of baptismal dipping, sprinkling, anointing, and washing with holy water sacralized by protective or healing charms pronounced over it.... When the (Christian) church adopted infant baptism, the ritual was promptly taken out of the hands of mothers and placed in the hands of priests, who claimed that all children were demonic 'children of darkness' as a result of passing through the female body and inheriting original sin." Hey, we can use knowledge and writing to reclaim what is ours.

There are some cultures such as the Laguna Pueblo people who felt stories held the sacred spirit of the people. To honor their stories and to tell them at birth and death, in times of joy and sorrow, gave honor to their histories and all times. When the cycle of stories was broken, so was the entire heritage of the Laguna, and the spirit was broken. The ritual of storytelling at all important functions held the tribe together with the past, present, and future generations.

In the novel, *Tonto and the Lone Ranger Fist Fight in Heaven*, the author, Sherman Alexie, demonstrates his character's unity with the earth in his writing, "Nobody dreams all the time because it would hurt too much but James keeps dreaming and sleeping through a summer rainstorm and heat lightning reaching down a hand and then a fist to tear a tree in half and then to tear my eyes in half with the light. We had venison for dinner. We ate deer and its wild taste shook me up and down my spine. James spit a mouthful out on the floor and the dogs ate and ate what they could find and the deer grew in my stomach. The deer grew horns and hooves and skin and eyes that pushed at my rib cage and I ate and ate until I could not feel anything but my stomach expanding and stretched full."

It is my wish that through the telling of these stories, and the deepening of your own connections through your writing, that you will better enjoy a rainbow or a tree with angel's wings in a storm. When you see two trees close together I hope you think of the Hindu tradition whereby trees were tied together in the hope for marriage and better fruit. I want you to be able to take a walk, notice the weather, and think of stories told and stories you could make up and tell.

HOW TO JOURNAL WITH THIS BOOK

In this book you will find fifty-two essays on the natural world—everything from mud to winter to moon to hair to dawn. At the end of each essay you will find questions to jumpstart your writing process. I structured the book so that it could be used weekly over the course of a year. If that suits you, great. If not, do whatever is comfortable. If you want to read and write on a daily basis, do that. Or every few days. If you don't want to keep to a schedule, that's fine, too.

The questions are designed to help you right where you are! You will find that depending on your mood or what you are working through at different times of your life, the text will have different meanings to you. For instance, if you are asked to think about clouds, on one day you might think of kangaroos hopping across the sky, on another simply be reminded of the changing nature of things. Today you might feel drawn to the way the clouds' long narrow stripes seem to be reaching for something. You might think about a bird and associate it with the sun, wind, and thunder gods with its lightning tongue. Or you might just think: "Ah yes, a bird. The spirit lives in tiny creatures." You might write about the beauty and danger in spiders and be glad for that awareness; life holds joy and despair in the same hand. By writing about the natural world, you will be reminded that you are part of the wise earth and all sentient beings.

When you've read the questions, just start writing and don't look up. Write in a stream of consciousness way. I call this way of writing *streaming* because, like a stream, it flows out of you. Don't look at what you have written. Send the judge and editor out to lunch. This is writing to help you get into a flowing state of self. As writing teacher Brenda Ueland says, "It is only by expressing all that is inside that purer and purer streams come." Write as fast as you can with a pencil and paper or zip across the keyboard on your computer and don't look back. You might start with ten minutes, and after a few days, try writing for fifteen and then twenty minutes. Try to write until you can feel that you have been in another mind-set where all is your breath, your fingers, and the words.

Sometimes we must write awhile to get to our truth. In the meanwhile, just the act of writing moves us closer to clarity that comes from our wise voice. You may find that choosing a regular time to write will help writing become a ritual to which you look forward. Also, a regular time to write becomes a structure or habit to count on. When you first wake in the morning, after a nap, after meditating, or just before bed, you are more connected to your subconscious knowing. It's called the twilight time. Try writing at all four times, and decide if you have a favorite time. More information will be available to you at these four times because the critic isn't as strong.

Journal writing is for our eyes only, so we do not need to remember grammar or proper punctuation. We are using our writing to drop us down into feelings, to make connections, not to show how well we know English grammar.

Let the mirror of words express what you are feeling. When I'm feeling happy, I write my joy in my journal as a reminder. I read essays when I want to learn and grow beyond my familiar way of thinking. I answer questions to explore how I feel. I write lists of gratitude. I write letters to my son and loved ones and tell them what I have learned from life, from them, for them.

When I feel unhappy, I wrap a cloak around me and wait for my ritual of twilight writing to ease the way to the unraveling and healing of my pain. When twilight comes, I bring out a special journal with a midnight blue cover and ask for release of feelings that feel hurtful. I imagine a spiral and how things start, how things happen. It's like a time line, only it's a feeling line in the shape of a spiral. I mark when I first started feeling badly about this incident on a spiral I draw in my journal. I find myself on that spiral and find my way down to good earth or up to the forgiving heavens.

On nervous days I fill my journal with nouns: dirt, rock, tree. Nouns feel solid to me. They calm me down. I continue in this vein on my daily walk, noticing nouns and saying to myself, "Water, egret, duck, wave, mud, grass." Soon I am enjoying the good bay smell and the feeling of stretch in my back. When I need to feel fanciful, I use lots of adjectives: gigantic, feathery, a frothing surf. I write sleek, shiny, shining.

Remember, you are not writing to amuse yourself; you are writing to find your life. You are using your writing as a tool to communicate with yourself.

Words brought me to a place beyond words, to the place of feeling one with the earth. It is out of this place that I write this book. It's for you and for me.

1. MUD BODY

"Oh mud mother, sister, aunt,
where are your white gloves and tiny shoes?"

JAN ALICE PFAU

A SCULPTOR FRIEND says that making mud pies is the closest she ever got to cooking. I know that following footprints in the mud when playing Sardines or Hide-and-Go-Seek is the nearest some of us ever got to becoming a private eye. There is something about mud that begs fun.

Mud was always considered a feminine material, sacred to women because it was their substance—earth—out of which their babies were made. Pottery has always been considered a woman's art because of this time-honored association.

In ancient myth, it was said that we emerged from mud. Tom Chetwynd tells us in *A Dictionary of Symbols*, "Mud is the malleable substance of our being, full of potential for growth and transformation."

Photographer Cindy Sherman often creates still lifes from objects found in the natural world. Her *Untitled #173* is a 5 x 7½–foot photo of dark and glistening mud. Look closely and what do you see in its deep brown body but mud, sticks, candy wrappers, a potato perhaps. It is gorgeous in its shine and detail and size. But is it garbage? Is it just mud of the earth with human life nearby? Is it a statement of beauty and ugliness living together? What she does is ask us to think of the symbolic meanings we associate with the little worlds she creates. It's as if she's asking, what does all this mean to you? Of course your particular associations with mud will make all the difference to how you answer that question.

I have always thought that my spirit lives closer to the mud than to the heavens. So many times as I live my life as a woman in this culture, I have wished to shed all the images of what I am supposed to be and just wallow in the mud. After many good rolls, I would shower outside and forget the uncomfortable shoes. I would be the woman I want to be: more authentic, comfortable, natural.

As a therapist I can see this desire to get down in the mud as part of owning the various aspects of ourselves—our need to be clean yet be "earthy"; our need to be strong and accept weakness; the knowledge that we are both good and bad, wrong and right. To be mature, we must learn to integrate these aspects into our unique selves. When we are honest with ourselves, we are aware that we hold these contradictions within us. Perhaps you can remember a time when you were aware that a wrong deed could have been done by you but for a bit of grace. This is an example of understanding the contradictions that live inside of you but are not necessarily acted on. It is a compassionate way to understand that any evil act could have been committed by you but for the grace of your wholeness and your ability to set boundaries with shadow impulses. That self-compassion shows that you honor your "mud self."

Mud is the part of us that can be shaped or molded. When we look at our life and see how difficult it is to change our patterns as we move toward more spiritual living and thinking, we can rejoice that we come from the shapeless mud and still have the potential of shaping within us. We can leave limiting and unkind beliefs behind and ask our spiritual self to help us live in flexibility and generosity.

Mud is often used as the symbol of the unaware man and woman. This is the self that comes from the earth but does not know sophisticated ways. This is also the self that is often seen as base and closer to an animal nature. We can incorporate the best of the self that links with the earth and animal ways.

Let us enjoy dirt on our feet and our instinctive nature. Let us enjoy a healthy lust expressed in sexuality. Let us be at home in the world of mud and earth and animal ways.

EXERCISES:

+ Imagine life being spun like a potter's wheel. What shape would the mud of your life take?

+ How do you envision holding "mud knowledge" as you develop on your spiritual path?

2. DAUGHTER OF THE CLOUDS AND STORM *(rain)*

> "Rain knows the earth and loves it well,
> for rain is the passion of the earth."
>
> ESTELA PORTILLO TRAMBLEY

I LOVE THE SMELL of the earth after a rain. The smell reminds me of new beginnings and fresh starts. That's what rain has always been about for me—new life for the garden, for crops, a time of tucking in to reflect. I like to use the sound of rain as a prayer, the sound a bridge between my body and nature.

The sheen over the pavement and the silver dew on the trees help the world show off its beauty. Outside our window rain may fall into the tin gutter, dirt softening the sound. Or, as we awake to the steady beat of rain, we might be reminded that we are part of nature and that nature is everywhere.

Rain is also a dance as beautiful as the one in *Swan Lake* where the ballerinas portray the swans in formation, their long, slender arms held high, bent at the elbow, fingers high, looking for all the world like swans' necks.

Rain's dance comes to me as the light under the swimming pool catches drops of rain like stars sprinkling souls over the water.

In a recent poem, I wrote about the effects of change and falling rain:

The wind and rain fly to the cape and bonnet
of earth. With sticks of rain like thread flying away
from the scissor-cut spool,
she sews moisture to the cloth of life.
Everything is on its way to somewhere, the rain whispers,

and like a youngster sharing wild cherries with summer birds,
    she enters the green grass of the world,
  her body a sail in the breeze.

Sometimes even with the desire to hold on to something nourishing, change comes and brings something different but nourishing!

A client once told me about losing her oversized boots in a fast-rushing creek after a downpour. She was so delighted she threw her socks in after them. If we're lucky, we still remember the excitement we felt about rain when we were kids and how much fun it was to play in warm rain and in the deeper creek beds it made. We may remember running back to the truck and eating a picnic in the cab, holding cups out the window to catch the glistening drops. I remember letting a rain shower take me in its arms and simply enjoying it. I also remember shrieking with laughter as we bundled up blankets and afternoon playthings.

As a child, I made a study of rain in different situations. There was rain that was like someone walking toward our playground all dressed up in light. There were pavements that were drowning, with small worms wiggling up from the earth to live. There was the rain that brought a rainbow, which made me dizzy with excitement because the colors beckoning felt like part of a magic story. Finally, I remember the torrent of rain beating the clothes on the clothes line my mother had hung out back, the clothes poles falling in the wind, reminding me to believe in ghosts and the power of the unseen.

In the language of symbols, rain is seen as life-giving, a blessing from the heavens. It has always symbolized divine favors and revelation or grace coming to earth. Once I gave an aqua-tinted jar of rainwater to a friend, Val, who was about to give birth to twins. The water was from a soft rain that fell several days before the twins' births. I wanted to give her a new way of baptism, and I wondered if the rainwater might hold a blessing for her babies.

I had a client who would light a candle to pray when it rained. She would pray for the grasses and crops and all that needed moisture. She would pray that there would not be so much rain that misfortune would come. She felt that a deluge of rain might be the wrath of the goddess asking us for better care of the earth, which is another ancient symbol of the rain. Most of all, she felt rain symbolized a time when the heavens were open to prayers from the earth and a time when prayers would be heard.

Hans Biedermann writes in the *Dictionary of Symbolism*, "The saintly abbess Hildegard of Bingen likened rain to the vital energy of the soul, which makes the body flourish and 'keeps it from drying out as the rain moistens the earth. For when the rainfall is moderate and not excessive, the earth brings forth new life. . . .' Hildegard also compared tears and rainfall. 'The spiritual person is so shaken with fear of the Lord as to break out in tears, just as clouds draw their waters from the upper reaches and pour it forth as rain,' thus the gift of repentance irrigates, fertilizes the soul, 'washing sin away.'"

Hopi Indians have their own special rain rituals. "The Hopi say that events are prepared and emerge from deep within the heart of all things, which is the heart of nature, of human beings, of plants and animals. This heart is not the physical organ but a subjective, inner realm. . . . Before events happen in the objective world of the senses, they dwell in the heart, along with thoughts and desires. The preparing may involve singing and dancing and/or other community ceremony events such as ceremonial smoking. Such acts serve to focus the thoughts and desires so that they can act as very real forces affecting the crops, the clouds, and the formation of rain. For a cloud is not a thing external to the human mind. It is an event that is in a state of getting later or growing, of transformation," writes James N. Powell in *The Tao of Symbols*. Rain is always in process: raining, about to rain, or living in our heart.

How enriched would our spiritual path feel if we believed that nature starts from within us, the weather simply an outside manifestation of that? The green growth after the rain a part of us? The rain itself coming from a need in us? Why shouldn't it be true?

Since rain is vital to life, much time in ancient cultures was spent summoning rain, often, as in Africa, by sympathetic magic. "The rain maker, magician, or shaman performs a ritual which imitates the effects of rainfall, in the hope that rain will thus be encouraged to fall. Examples of such methods include spraying a mouthful of water into the air as a fine mist; beating a victim until blood flows on the ground; quenching a fiery torch with water; or drenching member of the tribe with water. Other methods are to arouse the compassion of gods through the suffering of innocents," writes Alison Jones in the *Dictionary of World Folklore*. "If all else fails," she continues, "the folk may endeavor to force the divinity into sending rain by intimidation or abuse. When long prayers and sacrifice before a fetish or idol have come to nothing, the image may be torn down and exposed to the sun so that that the deity might feel for himself the agony of drought."

In *Dictionary of Symbols*, Jean Chevalier and Alain Gheerbrant write about rain as a symbol of fertility: "Rain is regarded universally as the symbol of celestial influences which the earth receives. It is self-evidently a fecundating agent of the soil that gains its fertility from rain, and countless agrarian rites were devised in dance form, in offerings to the sun, in Cambodian 'sand-mountains' or by using the smithy to summon a storm to send down rain . . . . Indra, the god of the thunderbolt, brought rain to the fields, but also made animals and women fertile. What comes down from heaven is spiritual fertility, light and spriitual influences as well . . . . In India, a fertile woman is called 'the rain,' that is, the spring of all prosperity."

We use rain as a charm the world over by wetting, splashing, and pouring water over people. It was once thought that witches could slap wet rags on stones to make the drops fly. Some Native Americans regard rain as a form of their ancestors whose spirits have gone into water or air, coming to visit or bring a message. Which of these myths do you respond to, and how does that empower you?

Here is a poem I wrote about rain and lightning that I named *Cathedral*. I thought it seemed like a myth of sorts. See what you think:

Cathedral

On the shell-like ruins of old foundations,
we built a lighthouse.
We hoped to grow old, keepers of rain and lightning.
Rain came first, the daughter of clouds and storm.
We fell in love with this wandering
daughter, called her Shiny Ropes, Sparkling Girl.
With her long strong fingers, she coaxed
fields into flax, crumbled rock into sand.
She brought illumination to watch over us
while she washed valleys and forests,
flat lands with her slanted pencils of hope.
Illumination kept vigil
signaling Shiny Rope's return
with a zigzagged flash across the sky.

EXERCISES:

✦ Write a magic story about rain and why it comes.

✦ How have you been a rainmaker for yourself, making things happen that you longed for? For loved ones?

3. ONLY GOD CAN MAKE A TREE *(trees)*

"Trees is soul people to me, maybe not to other people,
but I have watched the trees when they pray,
and I've watched them shout
and sometimes they give thanks slowly and quietly."

BESSIE HARVEY, *BLACK ART, ANCESTRAL LEGACY*

TREES ARE PART of the life cycle. We breathe in oxygen and exhale carbon dioxide while the trees breathe in carbon dioxide and exhale oxygen. They are the link between our soul and the earth. No matter where we live—city or town, farm or forest—we can have a favorite tree. I have had many: a maple, a willow, a dogwood, the avocado tree under which I first wrote poetry, and now a large pepper tree on the edge of the Emeryville Bay where I live. Each day, I walk north just far enough to touch its bark. If its leaves changed with the seasons, I would be blessed with that reminder of the earth's cycles. As it is, I study the pepper tree with reverence in the rain, with sunlight on its limbs, at twilight. The changes are there in more subtle ways than the seasons; perhaps that's similar to what has happened in my life as I mature.

For those of you lucky enough to live in a part of the world where there are changing seasons, the tree shows its gown in many ways: the thin twigs of winter or its ghostly skeleton covered with snow like cotton, the green silk of spring, the bloom of the summer's heat, and the flare of the rainbow leaves in autumn. To watch a tree transform in the natural cycle of seasons is a magical event in life.

I heard a shaman from the jungles of Ecuador speak the other night. He was asking us to help save the trees in the jungle by sharing in a ritual to call for protection from oil drillers and loggers. He called the forests in his homeland "the lungs of the land."

I often tell a tree to let me learn how to better be in the world, just be myself and let things alone. And I'll pray awhile. It's easy to talk to trees. Maybe that's because trees seem to be so at peace being themselves, with their deep roots and sweeping branches.

"It is such a comfort to nestle up to Michael Angelo Sanzio Raphael," writes Opal Whitely, "when one is in trouble. He is such a grand tree. He has an understanding soul. After I talked with him . . . I slipped down out of his arms."

Several years ago there was a show at the Legion of Honor Art Museum in San Francisco of Australian Aboriginal art that showed their sense of culture and spirit through their belief that all life and death is dreaming. The spirit of all things is in the dream. Their patterned bark paintings depict ancestors from the dream time. The tree is sacred, the land which holds its roots is sacred, the bark is sacred, and all are used for the messages of the spirit coming from the dream.

A tree feeds and nourishes your soul if you let it. Its branches reach up to heaven as if in supplication. Author Macrina Wiederkehr, in *A Tree Full of Angels*, writes, "Every time I meet a tree, if I am truly awake, I stand in awe before it. I listen to its voice, a silent sermon moving me to depths, touching my heart, and stirring up within my soul a yearning to give my all."

In almost every world religion and mythology, we find trees. As Alison Jones cites in *World Folklore*, in many traditions, they symbolize life and regeneration, "from the great world-tree of North mythology, Yggdrasil, to the Banyan tree under which Visshnu was born in Hinduism and the Hebrew trees of life and knowledge in the Garden of Eden. . . . Elsewhere trees were themselves objects of worship, and rituals were performed in sacred groves, and in Native American and African lore trees were believed to be inhabited by powerful supernatural beings or the spirits of the dead."

"Rooted in the earth but with their branches pointing to the heavens, trees are, like humans themselves, creatures of two worlds," writes Hans Biedermann, "intermediaries between above and below." The Tree of Life and knowledge grows in paradise right here on earth. J. C. Cooper writes in *Traditions of Symbols* that the Tree of Life "signifies regeneration, the return to the primordial state of perfection. . . . [It] also represents the beginning and end of a cycle. . . . Immortality is obtained either by eating the fruit of the Tree of Life, as with the peach of immortality in the midst of the Taoist Buddhist Western Paradise, or from drinking the liquid extracted from the tree, as the Iranian Haoma from the haoma tree."

James Powell points out in *The Tao of Symbols* that oaks, no matter how deep and solid their roots, are the type of tree most often struck by lightning: "In this respect they stand on common ground with the deeply poetic, prayerful attitude that is so vulnerable to bolts of sudden illumination. In European antiquity the oak was the most sacred of all things. In it the voices of the Gods were heard, and it was praised by the ancient bards as the granter of visions. These bards were something between poets, seers, and priests. . . . The oak itself rather than the vision it revealed became the holy of holies. To break a twig from a sacred (oak) bough was a sin."

In Judaism the festival of Sukkot honors God for caring for the Jews as they wandered on their way to the Promised Land. Festive huts are built of leaves of palms, myrtle, and willow: the spine, the eyes, and the mouth. These leaves are woven together into a lulav to denote the tents that gave them shelter. The lulav is carried around the temple as thanksgiving for their care.

In the Mayan culture, the Green Tree of Plenty will go with you after death and bring shade to paradise with you. However, you must keep rituals at its feet during your life.

I remember walking to high school through a cathedral of trees on either side of the street. As the trees touched overhead and made shelter, I felt like I was walking through a sacred place. And even with a fear of heights, I could not stay out of a tree, nor would I hesitate to build a tree house. I felt sheltered by trees. I once wrote:

She remembers days of somersaulting
her youth, hideouts
and the lifting of trees
believing the tweed of her life
was in the moving and always moving.

EXERCISES:

+ Take your journal to a tree, listen, and then write at its foot.

+ How could you use the nurturing voice of the all-giving mother, The Tree of Life, to better help you connect with a kind, gentle voice within you?

+ If a tree would reach her wide arms out to you and lift you to the sky, then lower you in her arms, how would your life change?

+ Is there a tree in life that has helped you? Write about how you might offer prayers for its healthy life.

4. THE BUFFALO EYE *(mountains)*

> "There came without warning a flower into me
> of that which I have come to associate with the gods.
> I went to the open door and looked up at the mountains
> with something akin to awe. It forced me out into the
> open where I could look up to the sacred high places
> on which humans do not dwell. Then it left me—
> perhaps to return to those sacred places."
>
> EDITH WARNER

AFTER A LIFETIME of teaching and tending to others, a friend of mine decided to have a last big fling and charge a trip to Europe on her credit card. (I have always loved her spirit.) She wanted to see the Matterhorn in Switzerland. As she gazed at the mountain, which moves up to a peak but in a gesture so sweeping it feels like there's an angled plateau at the top, she had an emotional vision of hope and possibility. She knew that the mountain contained life spirit. "I knew then that this wasn't my last trip after all, and indeed I joined an international choir to sing in European cathedrals the following year. The symbol of the Matterhorn helped me remember to *JUST DO IT*."

The next year she returned to Europe and sang at the Salzburg Dom, the major cathedral in Salzburg, where Mozart had been the organist and had written the music for the mass they were singing. She recounted, "The choir was placed to the left of the Sanctuary and the smoke rose from the censers swinging their blessing over the altar. The soloists were far above us on a balance that supported the organists. It was in a space so high in its vaulting that no words could describe the mountainous effect on all of us…the music, the cathedral

23

beauty and height, history in the air, Mozart. I felt like the Matterhorn was once again in my life and I was beginning my life again."

Robert Morgan in *Gap Creek* tells about mountains in Appalachian communities in the United States. Whereas visitors saw only poverty and backwardness, the mountain people felt rich on their own land with their families around and the old spring nearby. They were inspired by their devotional life and accompanied their hymns with banjos and fiddles. Most of all they loved their mountain whose cool nights and warm days held a spirit by which they lived. They knew of silence, where the singing waters started their flow, could feel the mountains as guardians of their life.

Mountains often make us think of the heavens. When a client described her impression at the base of the Himalayas, she told of their majestic size, as the mountains towered their way toward heaven. "When God gave men tongues, he never dreamed that they would want to talk about the Himalayas: there are consequently no words in the world to do it with," writes author Sara Jeannette Duncan. Awe, that's what it is. Majesty giving us the blessing of a focus beyond everyday concerns.

A winding trip through the Smoky Mountains shows us how much beauty there is in our country too. Miles and miles of green trees and bears! And as winter nears, preparation for the cold. "The mountains were getting ready for winter, too. They were very sly about it and tried to look summery and casual but I could tell by their contours that they had slipped on an extra layer of snow—that the misty scarf blowing about that one's head would soon be lying whitely around her neck," says author Betty McDonald.

I remember how small I felt on a trip to Yosemite National Park, as I stared up, not only at the height of El Capitan but at the way the mountain rose sharply from the ground. It was as if it had been sliced by a knife. I remember my sense of wonder looking up at the mountain and my sense of awe at the scale of such natural beauty. I once read how European travelers, as they first traveled across this country, shielded their eyes from jagged mountain peaks, as the wild effects of nature were not controlled enough for their comfort. Places like Yosemite ask us to open up and feel a greatness and perhaps consider the untamed parts of ourselves.

Mountains are history in the making. Standing in front of El Capitan, I wondered: What does it take to make a giant mountain? What really happened during the glacial age? And what has happened on this mountain through time? How many adventures and rituals has it held? How much life and death has it seen?

A poet friend, C. B. Follett, wrote that the rock of Yosemite is

> a plaything of the wind
> which has scoured it like hands molding clay,
> and it undulates in the kiln of the sun, its lovely folds and breasts and thighs
> drawing your eye, your hand.

I raised my son at the foot of Mount Tamalpais in Marin Country, California. *Tamalpais* means "sleeping maiden," and I always thought of the mountain as a seated woman holding treasures to share. I watched her with her head in the clouds and in sunlight. The changing colors of green and purple reflected the seasons as they passed through her life and ours. I always felt lucky to live at the base of this mountain, and I could feel the gods in us as we hiked her trails. In her anthology about Mt. Tam, *Beyond the Sleeping Maiden*, Follett writes of a seasonal blush of wildflowers and how it catches rain clouds and shakes them loose of their harvest. It's familiar and yet "rises sacred against the sky / holding something back, something for the gods in us."

In Jack Tressider's *Dictionary of Symbols*, we find the following listing under "mountain": "The spiritual peak and center of the world, the meeting place of earth and heaven—a symbol of transcendence, eternity, purity, stability, ascent, ambition, and challenge...deities inhabited mountains or manifested their presence with peaks high enough to be veiled by clouds. Such mountains were often fear as well as venerated—as in Africa. They were associated with immortals, heroes, sanctified prophets, and gods. Figurative mountains were usually envisaged as layered, representing the progressive stages of spiritual ascent. (The risks of scaling mountains unprepared were well understood.)"

Native Americans talked about the buffalo eye as the larger eye to better see your life. Being on top of a mountain gives us this kind of vision. "To rise above the treeline is to go above thought, and after, the descent back into bird song, bog orchids, willows, and firs is to sink into the preliterate parts of ourselves," writes Gretel Ehrlich. Mountains can help us sense the inner knowing of our bodies. It is a place to go to learn more about ourselves.

To some, mountains are unattainable, distant, unreachable. Others find mountains welcoming places. Overlook Mountain in Woodstock, New York, is sacred to the native people in that area, and they say that once in the shadow of Overlook, you must return. Something calls you back. "At a certain point you say to the woods, to the sea, to the mountains, the world, now I am ready. Now I will stop and be wholly attentive," writes Annie Dillard. We stop and see the sacredness in the mountain and honor that spirit.

I have heard from clients many times that when you grow up near a mountain, in some strange way it becomes a part of your family. One client, whose special mountain place takes the place of religion, nestles on her rocks in the pine in a visualization to find her wise woman. She feels a sense of spirit on the mountain more than she ever found in a church or cathedral. Her adoration and worship is of the natural world: the trees, the seedlings, the rocks, the bird's trill. She grew up with mountains around her in Denver, and when she wants quiet, she'll spend a few days in her high, green world. She reminds me of the quotation of Maria Augusta Trapp: "When you are a child of the mountain yourself, you really belong to them. You need them. They become the faithful guardians of your life. If you cannot dwell on their lofty heights all your life, if you are in trouble, you want to at least to look at them."

Exercises:

+ If you looked from the height of a mountain, what might you see about your life?

+ Sometimes we need to write to scare ourselves out of our everyday coping. How could you write about something frightening and have the mountains' support while you do this?

+ Mountains often seem to join earth and sky, the practical and the spiritual. What do you know about joining earth and sky in your life?

+ In the Hindu temple, the ceiling and central tower represented a mountaintop, the home of the gods, and the cavelike inner chamber, or *garbhagrah,* held the image of the gods. How does your spirit hold both the mountain and the cave?

+ How could you find a way to make the mountain part of your spiritual family and a homeland of your heart? Write about it and make it happen first on paper and then see if you can't create what you want.

5. DECODING THE CLUES *(intuition)*

> "Intuition is a spiritual faculty and does not explain,
> but simply points the way."
>
> FLORENCE SCOVEL SHINN

TRUSTING OUR INTUITION often guides us to do the right thing for ourselves. Becoming more intuitive means opening all our information-gathering channels. Messages may come from a look of surprise on a friend's face, a passage from a book, dreams, through the art we make.

I remember telling an artist client that I thought she should stop doing her art for a while. Her studio work hadn't been going well, and she felt she lacked talent. She was also giving her energy to a troubled relationship. The colors she was using in her paintings were messages about being muddy and unclear. I suggested that perhaps she wasn't connected enough to herself these days to explore her personal symbols in art. She was startled. She was a spiritual person who usually understood the larger picture. I could see that she needed to explore how her relationship was holding her back from her vision of life. She decided to take a break from her unsettled relationship and spend time with herself walking and journaling, seeing old friends. After a few weeks of distance from the turmoil, she had a better sense of herself and could see the relationship as disruptive to her sense of harmony. She was then able to untangle herself and, in time, her art took on a new sense of vitality and space.

The natural world holds messages for us as well. The robin is the first sign of spring in North America, and the fork-tailed swallow brings springtime to northern Europe. Crocuses poking up through the snow show the warming of the ground and the coming of spring. I was at a youth hostel near Palo Alto,

California, recently and I walked in the rain-filled woods with light falling on the green mosses of the trees and the lichen everywhere. It was February, and only the tiniest buds were on the trees looking very fragile as it softly rained. The ground was the rust color of vases made of this terra cotta earth. The message in the woods was one of everything growing and being fed and living at once. Beauty was on the ground and in the trees.

There was a parachute moss on the higher branches of the trees, weaving mystery. Every once in a while a blue jay squawked. The creek was full and made a wonderful rushing sound. I could hear both nature and silence in the forest and felt deep breaths of contentment.

It is at times like this walk, when my body is most relaxed, that my intuition is often most in play. I was walking in the woods but sensing that much in my spirit was living elsewhere. Part of my consciousness was in the rain forests of other countries, in the deep sea near Australia, in the mountains of Peru. Some mystics believe we live many lives at a time. I like to think of this and feel that there is much I am living outside of my consciousness or understanding. This is another dimension to the spiritual belief that I am all things and connected. The earth understands because she holds all of this growing and feeding and living.

Mari Marks-Fleming, a gifted artist who incorporates natural objects in a pattern using beeswax and pigments, has been doing art all her life and now, at sixty-seven, is being discovered; her work is selling around the world. One rainy afternoon recently she met with me at a café near my home in Emeryville and talked about nature and patterns and how even the collecting of the gingko leaves for her art is satisfying. In late November or December the leaves spread on the ground in their fall colors: she collects them in large plastic bags and dries them three inches deep on the carpet of her living room. Every day she sorts them by size and turns them over and over, which is a process she loves: the touching, the sorting, the repeating.

She collects from a favorite old gingko tree in Berkeley that has large leaves and a longer crack down the middle than most. She also collects from small trees in city containers in San Francisco, where she would find her smaller leaves with tiny veins. She said she had learned where to get each size and color of leaf, for the leaves never had the same DNA and were affected by the season, whether there was an early frost, or whether they came from an old or young tree. All of this was of great interest to her, and as she talked there was a lovely concentration in her manner as she remembered these trees and their magical meanings to her. It felt like reverence.

She also told me about losing her father in a fire when she was young. After that loss she turned to nature and swam out in a lake near where she lived in Iowa. She turned over on her back to watch the clouds and suddenly saw a picture of the whole world, how huge it was, how much sorrow and happiness she felt. Yet the world and nature just went on in their wise, benevolent way. "We struggle over little things, but they are our own problems. The world and life is bigger," she says. "It was not comfort I felt but just a feeling that even tragic events in life would roll on through a bigger pattern."

You might want to keep a journal of your intuitive feelings. Note when you get a message from the universe and what happens when you act on it. Also note what happens when you don't. Begin to recognize the feeling in your body that seems "accurate" and learn to trust that body feeling.

EXERCISES:

+ When and how has your sensate body calmed or alerted you? What was the message, and what lesson did you learn from this experience?

+ When have you or have you not followed your intuitive feelings? Sit quietly and pay attention to your body. Explore in writing what you think your body signal might be.

+ Find some natural objects and make some art. You don't have to know what they symbolize; just pick things that hold some power for you, as the gingko leaf did for Mari. Perhaps you could make a collage with some drawing or a painting that includes your natural objects. Enjoy the whole process by stepping into it like a meditation. It will feed your spirit.

+ Look around you today and see what messages lie at your feet. What messages meet you eye to eye, face to face? What hovers above you asking to be noticed? Write about this.

6. ALWAYS THERE IS A WHOLE *(fractals)*

"A person who believes…that there is a whole
of which one is a part, and that in being a part one
is whole; such a person has no desire whatever,
at any time to play God. Only those who have
denied their being yearn to play at it."

URSULA K. LEGUIN

I HAVE A FRIEND, Emilio, who has been living well and wisely with AIDS for fifteen years. Recently he moved to Bodega Bay, an hour from San Francisco, to live in a lovely A-frame cottage on a wonderful piece of orchard, farm, and forest land, with deer, wild turkeys, and grazing cattle living in harmony. There he rests and writes and enjoys the land and its harvest.

While I was visiting him one day, he took me on walk to an unusual site of evergreen trees all in even rows. It seemed strange to see nature so orderly, and he told me that this had once been a Christmas tree farm and the trees were planted in rows.

We walked beyond to a naturally seeded woods that was wild and uneven in its planting. My friend brought up the idea of fractals, how nature displays repetition of itself, the same shapes on a variety of scales. I thought of twigs and tree branches repeating their shapes. Also, the repetition of a leaf's vein design and the similarities to a tree's overall design. We talked of big puffs of clouds followed by smaller puffs of the same shape.

I remembered the ocean waves repeating themselves and the repeating shapes of the flames of a bonfire. A coastline with its big curves and little curves, its bays and harbors with inlets and lagoons in inlets becomes an endless repetition, or fractal, and a good example of nature continuing in the shape of itself. I knew I would write to find my place in this repetition of nature, and later in his tiny cabin we wrote and shared with each other.

One definition of a fractal is the whole containing within itself all parts of itself in like pattern. A microcosm reflects its macrocosm with splendid and infinite variations, much as humans do. We are ourselves and each other. We are unique, and yet we are part of the whole. We may look different physically, but we all are part of a design with feet, legs, torso, head, organs, skin. The universe can be contained in a grain of sand, and it is both wonderfully large and simply connected to the grain we hold in our hand. Our lives are like this: there is order in the chaotic quilt of our days.

Through writing and reflection we can begin to see how all the days of our life are connected to what we have lived through and what we have taken with us on our journey. We can see how the parts of ourselves make us whole and what connections have tied our lives together. In my life, the golden threads that have woven through every stage of my journey are curiosity, humor, and creativity. You may have an older family member who encouraged you, or an adventurous uncle or a literary aunt who helped you form a consistency in your life. Every life has a shape we carry and can honor.

EXERCISES:

+ How could your soul wrap around your body and bring you peace?

+ What helps you remember that you are separate and unique yet part of the whole?

+ When I think of ancient texts such as the Jewish Torah, I think of patterns of believing. Try to write down ten spiritual laws you want to follow in your life. Write these laws in pencil, symbolizing that you are not perfect but "becoming." Jews cover the Torah in a lovely cloth to reinforce its importance. Perhaps you can cover your book of spiritual laws with a special cloth, too.

7. THAT WHICH FLIES *(birds)*

"Sweet poet of the woods."

CHARLOTTE SMITH

WHEN I WAS ABOUT FOUR, I was told that robins left our cold snowy city to fly to a warmer home. When I then saw several robins in front of our house in the winter, my mother told me that they must have forgotten to fly away. I sympathized with these little creatures from nature and thought this was something that could happen to me. Daydream and forget, that is.

Throughout that winter I fed them apple pieces my mother had cut for me. I liked to see their big red bellies. One day my mother saw me run inside to get the kitchen knife. She was kind when I told her there was a dead robin out front and I wanted to get the apples back. She said I was half in heaven myself. I didn't get the knife or the apples, but those moments braided love, birds, and kindness for me.

Now, when I think of a robin, I recall that winter and how happy the robins made me. This is how personal symbols are made: memory, experience, and feeling. If I want to feel happy and connected to nature and my mother, I can sit and "daydream" or meditate with the image of a robin.

Birds also remind me that home is important. The first sign of the mourning doves on my patio came late this spring, after finch fledglings had flown away. I noticed a loosely made nest of sticks holding two oval eggs in my hanging geranium plant. I felt privileged to watch the consistency of care for their babies. The male sat on the eggs in the daytime, and at twilight the female came and stayed on the eggs until dawn. And at two weeks, the eggs hatched and the male and female again took turns sitting on top of the babies for warmth, their little beaks poking out at the side of the parent. (I could tell when the babies hatched because the adult bird began sitting very high in the nest.) I watched at different times of the day as both the male and female regurgitated "food milk" for the babies to eat.

I got great pleasure from this birthing on my patio. I relaxed, watching the harmony of the doves and how they cooperated by instinct. I found it soothing to watch the rhythm of care for their young. They helped me contemplate quietness and routine in my life and how that helps my spirit. I vowed to sit on the patio more often and let myself write a bit of time away with the mourning doves as my companions. Time for exploration, my space travel. (However, after three pairs of doves mated and used the nest on my patio, I got sick of the mess and said, "Enough nature," and shooed the next pair away. Yes, still spiritual.)

Joan Dunnings, in *Secrets of the Nest*, writes about hummingbirds building tiny nests over a brook or on a drooping branch, "Only about an inch across and an inch high, even with the female inside, the nest is indistinguishable from other knots on the branch. The female hummingbird builds her nest from materials that sound almost fairylike: over a core of bud scales bound to the branch with spider silk, she tamps milkweed fluff, fern down, thistledown, and fireweed into a contoured lining…the ruby-throat covers the outside of her nest with gray-green lichens, which she binds into place with more spider silks and the web of tent caterpillars. It is a miniature masterpiece, a padded jewelbox for two chalk white eggs no bigger than small beans."

My favorite (and only) nephew, Mark, collects hummingbird symbols to remind him of his relaxing vacations at his favorite aunt's house. (I'm his only aunt.) His east coast eyes help me appreciate the tiny hummingbird that hungers for its nectar, checking out my garden plants. Now that I've read that the hummingbird's speed is due to the large amount of sugar in the nectar, more than ever I think of a nest as a place where spirit rests, a place for the hummingbird to sit awhile.

A friend who had a lonely childhood remembers when she was eleven and she awoke with the early sun. She had airplane pictures pinned to her wall with one-inch metal pins. She saw the sun on her wall and the pins holding the pictures up in reflected light. A tiny bird flew in and sat on a pin, its little claws wrapped about the pin body as it leaned against the wall. It stayed a long time, and she didn't move; she wanted the bird to stay and stay.

Because birds are so plentiful, they bring nature and humor into our every-day lives. I remember sitting on a friend's back deck in San Francisco and hear-ing a phone ring. The hostess checked her phone and it wasn't ringing. The neighbors on either side weren't home, and their windows near us weren't open. Yet the phone sounded so close. Finally we realized it was a mockingbird in the pepper tree mimicking a phone, one of the city sounds it heard. One of the guests said she once heard a mockingbird make airplane noises and the beeping signal of a truck backing up. We have a trumpet player where I live. I wonder.

In Susan Milord's *The Kids' Nature Book*, she offers bird songs that sound like human speech:

Bird	*Song or Portion of Song*
Barred Owl	"Who cooks for you all?"
Chestnut-sided warbler	"I want to see Miss Beecher."
Ovenbird	"Teacher, teacher, teacher."
Robin	"Wake up, cheer up, cheerily up, wake up."
Rufous-sided towhee	"Drink your tea."
White-throated sparrow	"Ah, sweet Canada, Canada, Canada."

Notice the bird songs in your area and begin to identify the songs with the bird. Any noticing of detail will help you greater appreciate nature living nearby in your life and will enrich your day.

The writing in Peter Matthiessen's *Sand River*, the stories of natural life in West Africa, is a great example of how naming things brings things closer. Here is a passage from his book:

> I sat very still in the thin shade of a tree that grew from an ancient termite hill close to the shore. A brrt brrt of wings preceded the arrival of chin-spot flycatchers, and soon other birds came to the bare limbs and dead snags nearby; doves and rollers, a white-headed black chat, the lesser blue-eared starling, sparrow weavers, and a brown-headed parrot that could not make up its mind whether I was something it should investigate or merely flee. On one dead limb over the pool, two hamerkops peeped sadly as they mated; a pygmy kingfisher, turquoise and fire, zipped into a burrow hidden in the mound behind

me. Striped skinks emerged beside my book, and a parrot followed me all around the little hill, clambering along on the limbs over my head with electric shrieks of indignation as I stalked a very small deliberate slow bird, modest olive-gray above with pretty gray bars on a white breast, called the barred warbler. Searching for mites, the warbler worked from the base of a small bush up to the top, flew down and started again.

Doesn't it make you want to pull on your shorts, grab some suntan lotion, and hop on a plane?

Matthiessen's writing makes me understand why people travel around the world to experience the nature of Africa. He makes it come alive not only visually and in sound but through his rich, abundant details and naming. Do you ever remember being in a setting where nature seems larger than you, even in a small or intimate place? This is what his writings bring up for me. I remember personal symbols of Green Pike pond and dragonflies and red-bellied black birds playing in the heat.

Birds often show up in dreams and seem to embody the emotion with which the behavior is linked. A blue jay may represent a meddler, a chicken may represent either cowardice or domestication depending on how the client relates to the symbol of the chicken. Doves, of course, are often viewed as peace and harmony and even reconciliation. Sometimes *bird* and *flight* are the symbolic message.

Birds are like a spiritual magic given to us in the air and all around us to remind us of life. The southern Andean peoples believed that in the beginning the great creator gave black birds the right to fly off the mountain peaks to bring light back to the civilization that was just beginning.

Birds can also be dramatic and bring feelings of what it means to be free. I remember once watching wild geese flock across the sky, their excited voices moving fast across the growing darkness as they flew. It was a rare moment of a vision of wildness.

In mythology large birds are often associated with the thunder and wind gods. Their tongues are lightning. Birds in flight seem to be associated with our higher self or consciousness while smaller birds who fly close to the ground tend to symbolize our instinctive wisdom. The bird reminds us of our dual natures: tissue of earth and wings of the sky.

THE WISE EARTH SPEAKS

+ When you think about birds migrating, do you have a place that is more your home than others? How do you recognize home?

+ What would your life be like if you became a bird-watcher in your everyday life? How could it help you in rewarding yourself and in exercising patience. What else could you add with pleasure to your life?

8. TEACHING A STONE TO TALK *(rocks)*

> "For what is a woman's soul but a rock
> that can hold life solid and sturdy, a footing for dreams."
>
> JANELL MOON

WHEN YOU LOOK at a stone you can feel its ancient histories. Some of us know that stones can talk. They can lead you to self-knowledge and intuitive understandings.

There are many seekers who carry a special stone in their pocket for peace, or luck, or divine intervention, or for reasons they are not sure about. Some of us have noticed a stone as we were walking a creek bed and picked it up and felt a mystery awhile as we fingered its size and texture, and studied its design. A poet friend of mine, Kathy Barr, wrote that when she was young "[her] hands were bandits" when it came to collecting stones.

In Africa's Zimbabwe, the Stona stone sculptures have a wonderful history of talking with stones. After the harvest, the carvers sit in the dirt outside their imbas (huts) with a crude tool, perhaps a small iron hoe, listening to the village elders speak of their ancestors. With a vision deep within the mind's eye, a gift from the ancestors, they commune with the stone. They have no formal training and do no presketching, yet their work is amazingly unique in proportion and balance. "Let me go back to the roots of the Shona. You see in our tradition, there is a spirit called the water spirit. Let's say I have the form of the water spirit (in my head). I get a piece of stone. Then I start working with the water spirit, with the stone. . . . You see what will happen if it is the water spirit itself, the stone is going to come to me and say that it is the water spirit," says Lazarus Takawira in *Spirits in Stone* by Anthony and Laura Ponter. Takawire echoes Michalangelo's concept of "liberating the figure from the marble that imprisons it."

The ground floor of the San Francisco City Zen Center contains its vast meditation hall and its library, but few know that all the concentrated human activity down there actually revolves around nothing but one giant, placid rock. It happened that this rock was too big and too unwieldy, too hard and too deep to break into bits and cart away—considering the very tight construction budget the civic-minded Jewish women who built the building had in 1923. They had hired one of the few women architects in the world, the renowned Julia Morgan, to design a living space for young Jewish immigrant women displaced by the ravages of World War I. Here, in a "safe house," sixty women could stay while they learned English as well as the social and job skills of big-city life. So Julia Morgan, a woman of many harmonies, simply enfolded flowing halls and walls around the mountainous rock.

My writer friend, Celeste West, the librarian at the Zen Center, told me this story. She reports that the Temple Emmanu-El Sisterhood sold the building to the San Francisco City Zen Center in 1969 and that some of the good energy of the building may relate to the presence of this great living rock. She feels that the massive stone, receiving and emitting slow waves of energy, helps ground the Zen Center and all who come near.

Often in the spiritual life of a culture, a stone plays a part in holding the energy of the people. It may be a central stone either set in place or chosen because it is by itself on the land. The central stone was worshiped and used as the focal point of spiritual feelings. There may have been dancing and chanting around a stone to raise energy for the healing of their group and to bring the divine closer to their lives. Or there may have been a circle of stones to designate a place where spirit and matter come together in worship.

A stone can also hold energy for an important individual in your life. It can be your praying stone. When a close friend was going through a hard time, I started carrying one of the stones we had found on a vacation in Hawaii. She was happy in Hawaii. I thought of my friend and imagined the stone singing a song. I visualized women sitting on the cool stones at the water's edge rocking their babies. This would have been what my friend wanted, images of women in their ordinary tasks at peace with one another, a connection to nature sustaining them, a continuance. Now that she is feeling better, I am grateful that I thought to carry that stone.

A client, Colleen, was organizing a workshop for a group in a recovery house in San Francisco. She wanted to bring some ideas for self-care in early recovery when anxiety is high and hope is low. She thought about having these folks hold something from the earth in their hands, such as stone, and to go barefoot on their walks in the park.

Stones in the form of jewels are an archetypal dream symbol representing the treasure hidden in our unconscious. Ordinary stone symbols in dreams often mean we must infuse our life with more soul and spirit to give life more meaning. If we mine and care for ourselves, we may unearth that which drives our lives. One way to mine these treasures is to write and to work with our dreams. Another way is to do ritual, meditate, and write.

Artists have photographed rocks as geometric forms, rocks smoothed by water's time resembling the human body, or bedrocks wild and jagged reminding us of danger. Whether round as water-smoothed stone or jagged as anger, the rock life of our planet reflects our life and our soul's journey.

We use gray granite for tombstones at graves. Could the stone of the earth hold secrets of our life beyond and the spirit of those whom we have loved and who have died? If so, holding the stone may link you to your ancestors' and your coming spirit life.

A stone can be a reminder of strength and calm as well as connection. If we could bring back the ancient thought of life and soul in a rock, we would bring our connection to the wise earth closer. Our stone could bring us strength and calm by reminding us that we are part of a whole and that there are powers the earth wisdom has to share with us.

EXERCISES:

+ Get to know a special rock you find. Sit with it and come to know its form. Look at the patterns in the stone and see what the stone reminds you of visually. Imagine holding part of life's origin in your hand by holding your stone. What would you ask the stone? What would it say to you?

✦ Find a stone and teach it to talk. Decide on a current-day issue and ask yourself an open-ended question about it like *How can I find better balance?* Choose a stone that has enough surface so that you can see four visual elements in it, such as mountain, valley, crack, and circle. Determine how the "visuals" (gifts from the rock) are talking to you. An example from my four visual elements might be, *You can find better balance if you remember that extremes (mountains and valleys) may not be the attitude you need today. Look at the crack and see it as an opening to the circle of life.*

✦ Think of the earth's landscape and rock formations around you. How do they reflect or not reflect your life today?

9. EASE IN THE MEDIUM OF YOUR LIFE *(fish)*

"In a cool curving world he lies and ripples with dark."

RUPERT BROOKE

THE BASIC SHAPE of a fish can be drawn with two lines of a pencil. There's something about this shape that's intriguing, and it may be that once upon a time you doodled these lines in a classroom as you listened to a teacher drone on. Or it may be that the call of the waters came through your pencil.

With a little research, I found out that the design of a fish is a reflection of how superbly adapted fish are to the cooling, curving world of water. The fish's muscles produce the power to push forward through the water; the fish has the ability to do this because the weight of water allows the fish to live suspended effortlessly in it. A fish can swim its way cool and serene down the river or let itself be flung down the waterfall safe in its own element.

In the book *Trout Reflections*, David M. Carroll writes, "These speckled fish find places to ride out the hostile winter and perilous scour of thaw, they find springs and seeps and hidden deep pools in the time of low water, and they know the gravel runs with upwelling water in which they can spawn in the near freezing water of late autumn. These swift and cunning trout are equal to the demands of swimming the waters in which mink and mergansers hunt, and along the tree-lined stretches kingfishers perch throughout much of the year."

Just imagine what it would be like to be in your element with this ease. You would notice the bubbling creek and hear its sound. You would see the brown, dabbled rocks and note the grasses and moss and feel the soft mud under your feet. You would see the shadows of the trees, watch the cloud's shadow pass over the creek and realize that you were held in this beauty. The bearded trees of moss, your companions. The common sound of the woodpecker and jay would fill you with reminders of spirit, just as the late afternoon breeze brought soft kisses as air touched your cheeks. You would care about nature and its living as you cared about yourself and your loved ones.

I remember going to a duck pond at the bottom of the hill and feeding the ducks and fish. I was so very worried that I had overfed the "goldfish" because they were so huge. I was afraid they might explode. I never told this fear to anyone and so didn't learn they were carp, which are larger members of the same family, until I was grown. I was extremely careful where I threw my bread, however.

Today I find looking into a fish pond and watching the carp swim round and round very hypnotic and relaxing. I have a favorite place that has ponds, and I sit by them and dream. I do this before I start writing poetry and find that words flow better and seem more connected to the muse when written here. I think of water and sky and clouds and end up writing a poem about the petticoats of clouds. I am touched by the relationship of all things and realize the carp may feel the cloud's shadow as it cools its pond.

Nature writings helps us appreciate the world around us. Clare Walker Leslie and Charles E. Roth write in *The Alphabet of Trees*, "The developmental sequence in journaling usually begins with recording simple objects and events; in time it progresses to putting these objects and events into a context that stresses the connections between them. The accomplished journalist comes to focus on whole systems and their meanings to his or her life. Journaling can become a personal journey to a real sense of place and a holistic vision of the world." This is what you are doing by reading this book, taking the fish and letting it swim in its water and finding a way to love its doodled body on the pages of your life. We stop and consider how this creature reminds us to follow our own journey and asks us to keep waters clean for them and our children.

The caring of fish can remind us that everything is connected; all life is one, and we must care for small matters. Native fish are good indicators of environmental qualities and can serve as early warning of large-scale phenomena such as acid rain. For example, the tiny Delta smelt indicates the condition of the upper Sacramento-San Joaquin estuary because of its one-year life cycle. If their population is small, it shows that the balance of the upper estuary is in trouble.

Fish are extremely ancient and are thought to have been born at the very beginning of time when land and earth formed. Fish are usually symbols of life and fertility because they reproduce so rapidly with the vast numbers of eggs they lay. As gifts of the great mother earth, derived of her waters, fish are often symbols of the rich abundance of life held and offered to us. Because the ocean is so deep and fish can swim in the depths, fish can also stand for life in the depths of the subconscious.

I have a new symbol that daydreamed its way into my subconscious last week probably because I was writing this. I was gazing out of my office window at the bay trees across the street and all of a sudden I had a vision of a silvery, sparkling waterfall with fish joyously leaping over the falls. The feeling that came over me was abundant with the rushing sound and the fresh smell. I realized that there would always be more than enough for me. All I had to do was keep the stream fresh.

Just as we may see differently in the light of day than in the dark of the midnight hour, we see differently under the water. Symbolically, to see with "the fish's eye" is to see more into the psychic than one ordinarily would. There is a Chinese tradition of looking through a glass fish to see how the light shines through and to consider what you could know about a concern you are currently mulling over. Fish have been used in psychic readings to show when you are trying to find your way home; home in this sense is the spiritual world or the world of intuition. Also, because fish dart about, they are sometimes equated with streaks of intuition and intuitive flashes.

Hans Biederman writes in *Dictionary of Symbols*, "In many ancient religions fish were associated with love goddesses and the fertility of nature. But at the same time the fish is 'cold-blooded,' symbolically 'not governed by the heat of passion,' and for this reason is a sacrificial creature and particularly appropriate for sacred meals. . . . In ancient Egypt fish were eaten by common people but forbidden to ordained priests and kings. . . . This reveals our ambiguous attitude toward the deeper layers of the personality and their contents, which—like the snake—can be interpreted positively or negatively. Certain species are traditional symbols in Japan; the carp, for example, because it can make its way through eddies and waterfalls, stand for courage, strength, and endurance."

In *Traditional Symbols*, J. C. Cooper details how the Buddhists used the symbol of a fish on the footprint of Buddha to symbolize freedom from restraint and emancipation from desires and attachments. Buddha was also known as a "fisher of men." In Hinduism the fish is a sign of power and wealth and fertility and is an attribute of divinities of love.

Tales that speak of fishermen and their wives often show how it can be just as difficult to bring back the treasure from the sea (subconscious) as it is to find it. We read this in Hemingway's classic novel, *The Old Man and the Sea*, when all he returns to land with is the fish's bones, nothing to feed himself or others. Think also of *Moby Dick*, where Captain Ahab comes to grief with his efforts to return with the catch.

The salmon is a symbol of courage and determination. Salmon swim great distances against the river's flow to spawn and then die. In Celtic mythology this fish is associated with vision and inspiration because of its ability to find the way to distant spawning waters.

Exercises:

+ Think about insights as fish and the process of integrating new insight or awareness into your life. How is it difficult to bring "the fish once landed" into your life?

+ Seek out a glass fish and try looking through it for intuitive answers.

10. SWEET REST *(night)*

"The Earth rests, and remembers."

HELEN HOOVER

THE BALANCE OF LIGHT and dark in the skies can be a reminder for the balance we need in our lives. The skies can tell us to take note of how we spend our time, to rest and play, not just to work and sleep.

As a youngster I used to love to wake at night to hear the sounds of my family sleeping, my sister's breath, my father's soft regular snore heard through the thin walls. I liked the furnace turning on and off as a signal that it was cold outside and we were warm under our quilts.

Later, as a mother of an active toddler, the night was the only time I had to myself. I would wake in the night and make tea, read, and write for a few hours. I loved the quiet with my loved ones sleeping nearby. I listened to the trees touching the house in the night wind. Sometimes I could hear a high shriek of an owl. Most of all, I loved writing without interruption.

When my son was a little older, I lived on a wooden boardwalk on the Corte Madera Creek in Larkspur, California, where the shacks edged over the salt marsh that was an egret sanctuary. It was the darkest place I ever lived. I wondered if moonless nights were "double dark" because the land was so flat and still. Or if it was that here nature and the surroundings were so present that the dark really shone. I could hear the grasses whistle just a bit if the wind over the water was high. The creek followed the tides of the ocean and could drain, flood the marsh, or overflow the boardwalk. When it rained, I could hear rain all around.

In this tiny, two-room shack, I did the most vivid dreaming in my life: dreams of night movies with heroines dancing on bamboo trees and dreams of darkness that held great danger for hay fields and playing children. I remember an especially vivid dream when my spirit called me to lay huge red eggs in moss-covered trees that turned into snow-covered mountains. I woke up hearing the words, "Get your winter coat." Dreams of magic turned to literal practicalities.

According to the Hasidim, an ancient, pious Jewish sect devoted to mysticism, Mother Night gave birth to all the gods. She stood for the darkness of the womb, in which all things begin. If we pay attention to the night, we know that it brings good to us in creative ideas and dreams that lead to deeper knowing. An important part of our spiritual path is created in the darkness of night.

According to Jean Chevalier and Alain Gheerbrant in *Dictionary of Symbols*, "The Greeks regarded night (nyz) as the daughter of chaos and mother of the sky (ouranos) and the earth (gaia). Night also gave birth to death, dreams, sleep, vexation, friendship, and deceit. The gods often lengthened the night by halting sun and moon, so as the better to achieve their ends. Night moves across the sky, veiled as darkness on a chariot drawn by four black horses and followed by a retinue of maidens, fates, and furies."

Night is the image of the unconscious, and in the darkness of sleep the unconscious is set free. Night often symbolizes a time of germination, a time when dreams can come to light. It can be thought to hold all our potential, and we must go into the night to learn from the darkness, our nightmares, and our monsters. Like all symbols, night displays a twofold aspect—that of the shadowy world of the brooding future, and that of the prelude to daylight when the light of life will shine forth.

When we simply accept that part of our time is spent in darkness, we can bring our day and night into balance, allowing our day-mind to relax and our night-mind to reflect. "Night is the first skin around me," says Oneida poet, Roberta Hill Whiteman. Rather than feel terror in the unknown, we might feel protected by the night and trust in what we cannot see.

In a poem called "Wide Arms," about love helping us feel our spirits, I wrote:

Whether it is the warming day or the licorice night,
a spirit tugs at you while you turn
your head away. You know this is true
because you have felt it those nights
you lay steadied by love.

In the evening, without our even knowing it, our bodies begin to prepare for our dreaming time. When we write before bedtime, we have the opportunity to create a richer dream life, often finding that what we dream about is connected to what we wrote about before sleep. Meditating, visualizing a soulful future, or praying before bed helps. Light a candle to pray, and then write if you wish. Whatever you choose to do, end your day with some kind of recognition that you value the time of day when you rest.

EXERCISES:

+ Night is waiting to help you connect with deeper wisdom. What situation or feeling from today would you want to bring to your dreams tonight? What might you learn?

+ Try writing about two kinds of quiet: the "dead" silence that fills you with dread and the state of "alive" silence where something is going on between two beings. You might write about the time the angels from the four corners of the world came to your side and took the fluttering wings of your heart and put them to rest in a mound of deep blankets. You might write about "dead" silence being white and empty, while "alive" silence carries the colors of midnight blue and black so that it can hold all the joys and mystery of connection.

+ Let night enter and still your heart. Write about that.

+ What does night know about simplicity? What do you?

11. REBIRTH AND THE MANY MEANINGS OF BEES *(bees)*

"Float like a butterfly, sting like a bee."
MUHAMMAD ALI

BEES ARE PART of the good memories I have as a child making clover chains on a tourist house's lawn somewhere on the east coast. It was cooling to lie on the grass and stretch my legs after sitting all day in the back of a car. I liked the bees company in my solitary game of making nature's jewelry.

I remember lying on my back in a field overlooking the Mississippi after taking a salt shaker to the tomato patch at the side of my grandmother's house on a hill in Moline, Illinois. One of the strongest memories I have from vacations at my grandmother's is the buzz of the bee, the good, fresh smells in the air of mown and wild grass, and the sun hot on my back. This is when I learned that writing gives two lives: the one with the pencil in hand to linger over during cold winters and the one now living. Sometimes I recognized I was challenged to do something so I could write about it later. Ah, I thought in my not-so-young child's mind, I was creating more life.

It wasn't until three bees entered a soda can from which I was drinking one Memorial Day several years ago that I learned to guard myself from their venom. Three stings on the top of my mouth and left eye swelled closed. A trip to the emergency room. A change in feeling about the sweetness of bees. Something I didn't want to remember or write about but a reminder none the less that life happens, and we cope.

Once I had a neighbor who raised bees for their honey. Her little girl was a frightened and nervous youngster who was allergic to bees. I thought it strange

48

to take such a chance with a child's health and wondered what was really going on there. It reminded me of the makings of a Joyce Carol Oates story or something Anne Rice might use in a chapter called "Bees for Harm." I felt protective of that child and was glad to be her neighbor.

As in the spirit of all sentient beings, a bee is given specialized structures that help them gather and prepare their food: featherlike hairs for picking up pollen, pollen baskets and combs, tubelike tongues for sucking nectar. They actually taste nectar through their legs, which then act to spread pollen. Bees can also be respected because they are nature's most important pollinator, vital to plant and human life. Many cultures honor bees as a symbol of fertility.

The Greeks believed the souls of the departed entered bees. I was recently intrigued by a story that supports this idea written by my brother's girlfriend, Barbara Karthman, who hasn't read the Grecian myths. She writes about stepping on a bee on a day she called her Brahman Day, a day when everything was so clean and in its place that even the stones lining the driveway didn't seem dirty. What is so special about the bee in this story is that it started its life in Iran as a princess. Upon turning twenty, the princess escaped from her father, the Shah, to come to America. On the trip, the princess fell into a death state and became the bee on which Barbara stepped. The princess was used to magical things happening, so she didn't think it odd that she arrived to her destination as a bee. The sting in Barbara's foot completed the cycle of the princess finding her human form in the land that symbolized freedom.

Once I kept a small tablet in my purse and watched for a spiritual message each day. I'd jot it down and then in the evening explore the idea. Watching for a spiritual message and writing about it more in depth in the evening helped bring consciousness of spirituality to my life each day. It would be fun to start a "bee journal" and record messages from the sky to the earth and its creatures.

Bee keeping has been documented in Egypt as far back as ca. 2600 B.C. Humans have been gathering honey since prehistoric times, which helped the continuation of life. Honey's nutritional use has been long known. Honey has been used as a sweetener by queens and commoners. It's a marvel to see a honeycomb and the bee's activities and to learn of the queen and the drones. We can see a community of insect life working in harmony. We can use the community of bees and take some time to write about the challenges of belonging to a religious or spiritual community.

I have a friend, Jeanne Clarke, who, over the December holidays, invites her friends for scones and honey and a variety of teas. We sit in a circle munching and sipping and tell what we have been grateful for the past year. Then, we perform a new-year ritual. It's a lovely afternoon of appreciation with pretty china cups and the sweet honey. We, of course, are the queens.

Alison Jones, in *Dictionary of World Folklore*, defines bees as a cross-cultural symbol: "Traditionally (the bee is) a symbol of wisdom and industry in European belief. In Egyptian and Christian lore the bee is said to have sprung from the tears of Ra the sun god and Christ respectively. In ancient mythology bees were known as messengers of the gods, and in some places the tradition survives of telling the bees of a death in the household, so they can report it to the gods. In Ireland especially, bees are taken into confidence over any new enterprise, a superstition which presumably originated with the desire to secure divine aid, and in Scotland bees are proverbially wise. . . . In folktales bees often display a remnant of their ancient role, acting as God's spies."

In Egypt, honey from the bees was used as a preservative. The dead were embalmed with honey and placed in a fetal position to be ready for rebirth. Honey has been used for medicinal purposes for over 2,000 years. Provence in France is known as a region that makes honey oil. Last weekend, when friends and I were camping, Marjorie brought out "honey cream" to gently rub onto our faces to moisten and smooth the skin. Again, queens.

EXERCISES:

+ What do you envision as a spiritual community that would be just right for you? Who would be in this community? What would you have in common? How often would you meet, and what would the structure of your meetings be? Would you have a service element where members were helped in times of need? What would the challenges be for you?

+ How might you use honey to mark important occasions?

+ Do you believe in messengers between the departed and their loved ones? What is it that you believe about spiritual communication?

✦ When we think of community, we think of what we commune with. Consider the role of nature in writing (paper, charcoal, pencils, lead, inks) and art. Try writing an inspiration word or two with the stain from berries or on a piece of bark.

12. JOURNEY TO OURSELVES *(travel)*

"Certainly, travel is more than the seeing of sights;
it is a change that goes on, deep and permanent, in the ideas of living."

MIRIAM BEARAD

THROUGH TRAVEL, we learn about the earth's vast landscapes of hills and valleys, flatlands, rice lands, and seeded land. We can visit places largely untouched by tourism that show how the land and people live in their own true nature. There are still places in South America where indigenous people hunt their food with blowguns and live with their ancestors' ways largely unchanged.

Some travelers go only where there is water, and water is the beauty they seek: the lake, the wildness of waterfall, the ocean coating their ears with its ebb and flow. They roam to the island of Bali to explore a spiritual, artistic culture. They feel the possibility of living a life valuing the land, art, and their gods and how this braiding can be a daily thing. Or, they choose a lake nearest to their home to swim in the expanse of blue.

Travel can be a creative act that feeds the imagination and asks us to wonder about ourselves in a new way. When we are privileged to attend a tree frog ceremony in Africa, the day when the frogs come out of the mud signaling spring and new life, we see how other peoples honor the changing of seasons. We can also be close to the earth and let it help us recognize changes in the season of ourselves.

After a journey to Thailand, we may want to make our own "safe houses" so that spirits that are alive in the world can have a place to go rather than come into our family dwelling. Just in case the spirit brings trouble! Or, after a trip to Mexico and attending a family ceremony of initiation for a fifteen-year-old girl from childhood into womanhood by giving her a white dress to wear and allowing her father to change her shoes from the shoes of childhood to the shoes of adulthood, we may want to do an initiation for our daughter or ourselves. We might decide to bring her friends together and have them light a candle and talk about what was best about childhood and what they now look forward to experiencing in adulthood. The initiation doesn't matter; what matters is that we give ourselves and our children acknowledgment of passages.

"Through travel I first became aware of the outside world; it was through travel that I found my own introspective way into becoming a part of it," writes Eudora Welty in *One Writer's Beginning*. Who are we now that we have had this experience of travel? The historical sights may give us a greater sense of time and history and appreciation for the earth and its peoples. It may encourage us to learn a new language and develop an interest in the people of the land.

A client, Yolanda, who taught English as a second language in the mountains of Cambodia, found that students there are expected to help each other on tests. From their point of view, they help the less able pass the test. Cheating is not a concept they understand. At first Yolanda was surprised, but then she found it a relief to live in a culture that was not based on valuing competition. She changed her teaching methods so students could help one another all the way through the process of learning English. Yolanda went outside with her students at breaks and sat quietly under the Bodhi tree to rest just as Buddha had done many centuries ago. Together they honored community and their physical environment and the everyday connections people and nature gave them.

On her return from a year in Morocco, a student told me she would always remember the sunlit buildings in golds, tans, and pinks as her first memory of Fez. Just as the natives of the land, she determined her daily activities taking into account the intensity of the sun during the hot season or because of the particular time of day. To live being guided by nature was a major change in her life, and at first she felt held back by it. Gradually, she accepted it to be the truth as it was: the sun was the director in many cases. Finally, she felt blessed that she had lived that year letting the sun guide her. She found she could better explore her spiritual nature when she was not so consumed with controlling her life.

The wanting to travel is often akin to the wanting to write. Travelers often want to create a world to live in. They live a lifestyle awhile that is curious, questioning, open. They take these qualities to the page, and their hand draws a trail of inked recordings, memories that shape their clay bodies and ours if we too are open. We read of the way travel gives them a full life about which to write. Sometimes this forces consciousness. Sometimes, as readers, we say, "Ah, I knew that and here is confirmation."

Sometimes vision and travel leave us with a visual memory or diary that enriches our lives. I had a student who, as a child, lay on the grass in her small town in Utah studying the sunlight on the blades of grass. She studied grass at every time of year and every time of day until she could draw grass lit in various ways without seeing the scene. She knew how every ripple of wind affected the turning of the grasses. She learned to depict that in oil pastels and paints. The basis for her travel was her imagination, which allowed her to travel into the subtleties of light and form, the subtleties of the earth. With this concentration, she could see her world with awe and appreciation wherever she found herself. She brought this enthusiasm to everyone she met and enriched their lives with her passionate energy.

Exercises:

+ Why not look back over the traveling you have done in your life and determine how a trip affected your life?

+ How has travel within yourself been a beautiful drawing?

+ Rent the video *Crouching Tiger, Hidden Dragon*, shot in China, and write about the poetry of movement in this movie. Do you believe the young woman's belief in herself would allow her to travel to a new life on the other side?

13. THE SPIDER'S PARLOR *(spiders)*

> "When I'm hanging head-down in my web.
> That's when I do my thinking."
>
> E. B. WHITE, *CHARLOTTE'S WEB*

I REMEMBER loving the poem *The Spider and the Fly* and asking my dad to read it to me over and over again. It was one of my first introductions to intrigue and capture, and I found it exiting. Then I learned that although all spiders have venom glands used to paralyze the prey they trap, very few are harmful to humans, and I was somewhat disappointed. I would watch the spiders my mother's broom has missed in the ceiling corners and get a glimpse of what my mother called "the hardship of nature" as the spider caught a fly.

The spider comes in all sizes and shapes. The smallest is the size of a period on this page and the largest can eat a bird whose leg spread is the width of this paper! A spider always spins a silk thread, called a dragline, behind itself as it moves about. When threatened, it can drop to safety from the dragline. The spider's care from its maker! Sometimes knowing more information about a spider and really noticing dampens any fear you might have.

In many different cultures, the spider is seen as a heroic "mother" symbol, the spider web itself symbolizing destiny and mortality. In Jack Tresidder's *Dictionary of Symbolism*, we learn that spiders "can symbolize either ensnarement (by the Devil in Christian symbolism) or protection from storms, as among some Native North Americans. Folklore associations of the spider with good luck, wealth or coming rain are widespread, a symbolism that may be suggested by the spider descending its thread, emblematically bringing heavenly gifts."

In *Dictionary of World Folklore*, Alison Jones explains the healing powers of spiders: "A spider in a silk bag was carried as a charm for health. . . . The web of a spider too was thought to have curative power applied to a wound; this is actually quite logical, since it helps the blood to coagulate, although the web is sometimes rubbed into the wound rather than simply held against it, implying a belief in its intrinsic healing properties, encouraging the skin to knit and heal by sympathetic magic."

Jones continues to explore the theme of spider as savior: "A common motif of folklore is the spider who saves a fugitive by spinning a web over his or her hiding-place; the pursuers pass by, thinking that no-one can have entered the cave recently. . . . A variant tale tells how the Scottish hero, Robert Bruce, despondent in his cave, was encouraged to continue his fight against the English by watching the patient efforts of a small spider spinning its web."

There are symbols of the spider used in many other important ways. Throughout time the spider is not a creature taken lightly! In psychology the spider has been used as a symbol of introversion and narcissism, where the individual is swallowed by his or her own center. Buddhists believe the spider is an illusion because its soul is empty of being. Of course, witches are know to use spiders in their brews.

Because the spider is both fascinating and frightening, it is an interesting symbol about which to write. Learning what the spider means to you may take you another step on your spiritual path. When I write about the spider, I realize that I am reminded of wit, capture, and freedom. My writing details the feelings trying to stay separate and yet connected to others. My writing becomes an exploration of the self looking for a spiritual home and the need for connection.

EXERCISES:

+ Try writing about the feelings the spider evokes and see what you come up with that might be useful to you on your spiritual path.

+ How could you be the creator of joy sitting at the center of your web? How could you include others?

+ What role has both fate and free choice played in your life?

14. BEAUTY FROM THE TEEMING POND
(lotus flowers)

"Om mani padme hum."

FROM A TIBETAN PRAYER TRANSLATED AS,
"OM, JEWEL IN THE LOTUS, AMEN."

THE LOTUS FLOWER blossoms in white, pink, or pale blue, and it is found in fresh waters throughout the world. In ancient Egypt, the lotus was believed to be the first flower, blossoming on murky waters with such beauty that it was easy to imagine it to be the very first sign of life. In Egypt, the Great Goddess was called The Lotus because the sun was born from her at dawn. This was partly because the flower opens in the sun and closes at nightfall.

The lotus roots lie in the bedrock of a pond, the stem grows up through water to come to the surface where its blossom lives on air and sun. Significance is associated with the lotus in various cultures, as noted in *Dictionary of Symbols:* "The major writers of Hinduism make the lotus a symbol of spiritual fulfillment from its rising out of the darkness to blossom in full sunlight. From the Buddhist point of view, the lotus—upon which Shakyamuni sits enthroned—is the Buddha's nature, untouched by the polluted atmosphere of *samsara*. . . . Japanese literature reduces the symbol to a more commonplace level by frequently making the lotus, flowering unsullied on the muddy waters, an image of moral standards maintained unsullied and unaffected by sordid waters."

The lotus was taken as a symbol of the four elements—earth, water, air, and fire—with its feet in the earth, the water supporting its growth and stalk, and its blossom to be nourished by air and sun. Fire is symbolized by sun and is a further symbol of the lotus, one of fertility energized by the sun.

The lotus is often seen as the highest form of knowledge, or spiritual knowledge. In yoga, the currents of energy rising through the body are often symbolized by the bloom of the lotus on the crown of the head. In Taoism, the highest lotus is similarly the golden blossom of the lotus. In China, legends center on the lotus and its birth from the mud but arising as a symbol of aspiration in its clean, fragrant bloom.

I have used the lotus in poetry to symbolize the different stages of our relationship to ourselves and each other. These stages are represented by its birth in the earth, the rising of the stem, the learning time of the unconscious in the waters of our soul, and the blooming of self knowledge. The stages are both sequential and on going. There is a time for each stage and a rocking back and forth. Each stage has its overlapping and moving forward to the light.

There is a pond in Golden Gate Park in San Francisco that has white lotuses growing. This pond provides solace. Because the lotus shows in its example of living all of life's stages at once, I am better able to accept how I am both aware and unaware, both kind and unkind. I see an example of growing and holding on to the bedrock, grasping and letting go. It shows that I can blossom and yet be afraid at times. It is a flower that helps me understand and forgive myself.

The lotus also symbolizes the past, the present, and the budding future since it bears buds, flowers, and seeds at the same time. It is a symbol of what we hold inside ourselves at any given time.

The Egyptians and Hindus believe the lotus also symbolizes the creativity of life. She is the flower that was at the beginning; the sun rose from the lotus at the beginning of the world. The lotus is beauty and the beginning of all existence. The seed pods generate seeds that are released in the spring to put down tap roots wherever the waters carry them. This symbolizes that we carry creativity wherever we go.

In Chinese Buddhism there is a belief that after death the paradise of the soul becomes a lotus on the sacred lake of death. When the lotus opens, the soul is released into the presence of the spirit or God. In a movie from Viet Nam, *Three Seasons*, I saw this belief portrayed. An old man died and was gently laid in a small boat. The body was covered with lotus flowers and the boat was sent to drift its way around a pond filled with lotuses. It was a beautiful image of finding your way home.

If you don't live in a place where lotuses grow, you may be able to find a picture of this lovely pond flower and meditate with its image in front of you. Its long history may give you peace and the opening of your own spiritual nature and the creativity that is held there.

EXERCISES:

✦ If the lotus flower could lend you her creative force, what would she do for you? Write your answer in a poem.

✦ Where would you go if you could have a nearby "special place" to dream and write? Try it out.

✦ Why not start a nature notebook, something you can keep in the car for your pleasure? It will help you develop the art of "close-seeing" as you take a walk or enjoy a sunset. You might buy some colored pencils and add simple sketches to your words. One way to start is to look for designs in nature such as how flowers are arranged on a lily pad or how the rows of planted crops make a pattern on the landscape.

15. THE BURNING HEART *(sun)*

> "The sun, God's own great shadow."
> JULIA PETERKIN SCARLET SISTER MARY

WHEN THE SUN IS OUT, I want to run toward it and be held in its warmth. Suddenly, I take long walks and bicycle. I open the window and let the sun and fresh air spread over couches and beds and my skin. I spread sheets out on the line and smell freshly dried cotton. The urge to garden swells up, and I hurry off to the nursery to get seeds and grow plants with blossoms.

I had a client whose father recently died, and she missed him very much. He had loved her well as a child and had been able to give her love, understanding, and guidance. She said that all her life she had felt he was with her holding her hand, even though they had been living in different countries the last five years. The only thing that helped her in her grief the first months after his death was to lie down on the grass in her backyard and let the sun do its magic. The late spring heat made her feel connected to something good and warm, reminding her of her father.

Because the shape of the sun has usually been associated as feminine, when we look at the sun, we can use it as the muse for the feminine. In Hindu the sun means "unbroken circle with no circumference." The Hindus say it's nowhere and everywhere. Our subconscious may remember a circle is equality rather than a hierarchy, and we may find ourselves drawn to the cooperative spirit; we can then imagine what our lives would be like if we felt encouraged to flourish. And what if we lived in an atmosphere of cooperation and equality?

We learn from Hans Biedermann's *Dictionary of Symbolism* that "Countless religions associate a sky god with the sun, and there are countless names that designate this sun god as the destroyer of darkness. In one Babylonian formulation, the sun god is addressed as 'you who illuminate darkness, light up the heavens, and annihilate evil above and below.' Japan is actually named for the sun. The Japanese word for Japan, Nihon, is made up of elements meaning 'sun' (*ni*) and 'source' (*hon*); thus the country is often called 'the Land of the Rising Sun.'"

The sun has varied influences on the earth. The sun is the source of heat and life, and its rays represent the celestial influences that the earth receives. However, the sun can also cause drought and bring much destruction to a people and their crops. The Chinese believed that too much heat from the sun could be destroyed by shooting arrows at it.

We can look up, remember the sun, and absorb the gift of warmth we are given. Awareness can connect our lives to nature no matter where we live. We can have inspirational thoughts and experiences just by living in tune with nature. We can write our gratitude for the brocade of gold that sometimes offers our lives its weaving.

When the sun is not out, we can bless the unseen and know there are things beyond our awareness. We can write and pray for what is yet to appear in our lives. After sunset we can bless the sun as the Black Sun in her journey, leaving our world to shine on another.

Light symbolizes spiritual awareness and the ability to live a life of kindness. We hear expressions indicating this, such as "I came to the light" or "She could see the light." Once we have an awareness, it will shine in us forever, for there is no going back.

As the heart of the world in many traditions, the sun is sometimes placed in the center of the wheel of the Zodiac. If the sun is the heart of the world, just to let it shine on us could remind us to live in our heart and to let our emotions respond to the world.

EXERCISES:

+ When the sun reaches out her warm hand and touches you, how can you write her your gratitude for the comforts you have in your life?

+ Explore how you can be excessive like the sun in your intensity and how you can hurt those you love in this way.

✦ Your spirituality may deepen its intensity for you if you have a sacred place set up for yourself at home. Why not set up an altar of a flower and candle and incense? When you light the candles, the smoke from the flame and the smoke from the incense wafts the truth toward you and carries your devotion into the spirit heaven. It can be an altar with a sun sign, a special stone, and a feather: heavens, earth, and the air between. Whatever you choose, it can be your place to write special prayers of comfort and hope.

16. THE TWIN SELF OF FIRE *(fire)*

"Fire is the natural symbol of life and passion,
though it is the one element in which nothing can actually live."

SUSANNE K. LANGER

THERE IS NOTHING like a fire to take us to our spirit. Because of this, fire can be a really good companion. If we've been lucky in our life, we've had the opportunity to sit by ourselves and dream gazing into a fire. Fire can lull us into a meditative state where we can feel the pictures the fire brings: flaming antlers, candelabras, hands in gloves, spirits calling. Perhaps fire holds memories around the campfires of our childhood, the youngster in us who was fascinated by heat, flame, and destruction. Perhaps you can take your questioning self to the solace of the fire as it flames its heat and explore your questions.

Fire can be used as a metaphor for that which destroys what it feeds. The days of sexual flame are days in which it is hard to find balance. But who would want to miss those days! Fire is sometimes needed to feed our lives and to help us find our loves; a smaller fire may be stoked to make our dreams come true, not the blast furnace of beginnings. We find that the moderate path is the path on which we can live with joy and serenity.

When we think of symbols for healing, we know that the geometry of fire speaks to our spirit. The jagged edges tell of anger or anxiety, the leaping flame of movement, the crackling sound of transition or unrest, the rounded edges of mellowing. So too in Buddhism there is a belief that energy flows upward until it transforms into spirituality: earth to water, fire to air and release. As we gaze at a fire, we are symbolically watching fire flow into air to the spirit.

In *Folklore, Mythology, and Legend,* Maria Leach says that "throughout the world, from South America to Austrialia, Africa to Europe, Asia to North America, the myths indicate that the original fire of mankind, stolen usually from the gods or from some other previous owner, was hidden in the trees or in a specific tree, and that ever since man has had to rub this wood to produce fire. The general Polynesian myth, for example, is typified in the Maori myth of Maui, who went to his grandmother, Mahuika, the goddess of fire, to obtain it. She produced so much fire, from her fingers and toes, that everything began to burn. The rain put out the fires, but still it remained in some of the trees, from which mankind ever since has been able to get fire."

Another well known myth that came out of Central America and Europe is the tale of the phoenix. This creature, half eagle, half pheasant, sets itself on fire every hundred years and then rises after three days, rejuvenated, from the ashes. The phoenix symbolizes life everlasting and a spirit that will not die. Often after loss and transition, we may feel like the phoenix; we have seen our lives eaten, yet we rise again, wobbly sometimes, but on our way to healing and willing to risk again.

There are countless passages that tell when agrarian cultures set fire to their fields; a purification by fire, they were bringing the living green back to the worn earth. You can reflect over your life and determine times you have been reinvented from the ash of life's experiences.

The festival of the summer solstice remained a major pagan holiday. The solstices and equinoxes were important festivals, in harmony with the growing season so necessary for their survival. Midsummer was the time when the sun reached its peak and would now start its journey toward winter. At midsummer, burning a huge community bonfire was a signal to the sun goddess to come back for the crops of the next spring and summer.

Fire often signifies the fervor of religion. This can be positive or negative depending on the kindness involved and the respect for diversity of people and thought. The circle of fire is often associated with chastity, a state in which the young need adult protection.

EXERCISES:

◆ What fire myth do you relate to and how can you use it?

◆ How can you use the fire of anger in a compassionate way to stand up for yourself?

◆ Where does your fire passion live in your body and how can you access it more regularly?

17. THE WIND'S TOUCH *(wind)*

"The wind is like a great bird tumbling over the sea
with bright flashing wings."

KATHERINE MANSFIELD

As a child I memorized Christina Rossetti's poem, "Who Has Seen the Wind?" which talks about the wind passing by even though we don't see it. It reminded me that what we don't see can still be real and helped me believe in my dreams and my spirit. I was always looking for reinforcement for the belief in the unseen. I responded to the sense of magic that the wind brought with its invisible presence. The wind was intangible, transient, elusive, but there was no doubt it was there.

I remember a neighbor lady telling me the wind brought a spirit kiss to my cheeks. As I struggled home in the snowy cold, I would try to pretend I was being kissed, but sometimes I could only cry. Then I read in a Christian myth that winds are the messengers of the gods and can indicate the presence of a god force. I felt the force both in roughness in winter and sweetness and cooling in summer

For many religious and spiritual teachings, the wind is the vital breath of the universe, one of the only things, along with water, that was here when the world was created. It was a force before our human nature came into being, and it can link us to the creator and beginnings. Imagine yourself as a new force on the earth and what you might feel about the wind. Imagine your soul knowing you as good and innocent and what your feeling would be toward a problem you have been gnawing at in your life.

Spiritual energy, often symbolized by light, can also be symbolized by wind. Imagine the wind stirring the treetops announcing the spirit's coming. Wind can also bring blessings, hardships, and teachings.

In dreams, wind often means that change is coming. When a storm gathers, it may be the coming of a great movement in you. A gentle breeze may be the healing of difficulty. Eastern cultures seem to understand the significance of the empty space in which the wind blows and which, paradoxically, they regard as a powerful symbol of energy.

There is a story in Elan Golomb's book, *Trapped in the Mirror*, that tells of how the Buddhists used danger and the wind to make sure the monks were not too full of themselves and were actually ready to serve others in a compassionate way. They had a tradition where these Tibean monks constructed "box kites in which they stood erect and flew on air currents over vast depths of sky. If flying made them arrogant they would unknowingly shift posture and some would plummet to their deaths." Thank goodness we have more chances than that, but we too can use the wind to remind us that we are part of the whole: the weather, the angels, the human on the edge of the world who suffers.

EXERCISES:

+ If you know your restless days are the winds of tomorrow blowing their way to you, how could you enjoy today?

+ Write about the importance of empty space before the wind comes to feed a beginning in your life.

+ What blessings could the wind bring your loved ones?

18. SEEDINGS *(seeds)*

> "The kingdom of heaven is like a grain of mustard seed,
> which a man took and sowed in his field; which indeed is the
> least of all seeds: but when it is grown, it is the greatest
> among herbs, and becometh a tree, so that the birds
> of the air come and lodge in the branches thereof."
>
> MATT. 13:31.

MY FIRST MEMORY of seeds is from the story of "Jack and the Beanstalk." I was entranced by the idea of magic seeds. Imagine a plant so high it could be climbed to take you to another world. I loved the story up to this point and then lost interest. I wanted a kind world, not the world of theft and danger, win and lose. I daydreamed about a world grown from seeds that would please me. It was a landscape of children and magic happenings at every turn: pumpkins that talked, houses that went with you and waited for you as you played, dogs that fetched money and chocolate marshmallow hotdogs, large families in palaces where the children were free to live on their own floor with private exits and entrances.

Growing up in Ohio, the Buckeye State, there were huge, spreading buckeye trees everywhere. The thick pods would drop and open to reveal the gleaming mahogany buckeye holding its pocket of seeds. The neighborhood children and I would gather them up and put them in our laps. We would admire their beauty and want to do something with them. We were told they were poison and not to eat them or drill into them to make jewelry. It was one of the first times I learned that it's okay to put something in a bowl and enjoy it for its beauty. I do remember being quite young and going door-to-door and selling them for a penny apiece to kind housewives until my mother asked me to stop.

There's a great list in Susan Milford's *The Kids' Nature Book* that helps us understand how seeds get around:

Helicopters
Maples
Elms
Ashes

Hitchhikers
Burdocks
Cockleburs
Beggar's ticks

Parachutists
Dandelions
Milkweeds
Thistles

Delectables
Apples
Cherries
Berries

Floaters
Coconuts
Cranberries
Lotuses

Missiles
Jewelweeds
Witch hazel
Wood sorrels

I liked the names she ascribed to the various ways seeds pollinate and thought you would too.

In the spring, notice the way seeding happens outside your window. You might want to write a poem using Susan's list, since poetry is best in specifics, and noticing is a way to bring you closer to nature and your origins. Your poem might tell why the new seed needs to leave the "mother" in order to better survive and how nature helps it do this.

We can think of seeds and the seasons: how in spring the seed is planted and waits for summer for its full growth and flourishing with the help of sun and water, in fall the seed readies for its return to the rich earth for rest and renewal. Winter is a time of waiting for new ground. Snow can be seen as the blanket needed for the warm, deep sleep of the seed.

The seed's journey can be a metaphor for our spiritual life: times of growth and times of dormancy that create a circle, a whole experience. The "Homeric" hymns allude to seeds that die and sprout as life and death, with death living in realms below the earth and life in the light of heavens.

EXERCISES:

+ Draw a time line of your life and show how your life would be the seasons or the "Homeric" hymns. There would be times of action, natural or forced endings, times of dormancy, and times of new beginnings. Walk through your world for a day thinking of yourself as a "new seed" and decide how it feels.

+ What are the different ways you could unleash the seeds in your body that want to write?

+ What is your belief about the beginning of time? How do you fit into this and why are you living at this time in history?

+ Use the *gazing into the waters* technique, where you quiet your mind by noticing your breath and body and then let yourself drift to a world you would like to live in today. (Writing techniques are further detailed in my book, *Stirring the Waters: Writing to Find Your Spirit*.) For me, I'd like to find more seeds for a creative, spiritual community that feeds my life. What would it be for you?

19. THE GENTLE WORLD *(cows)*

"There is nothing stronger in the world than gentleness."

HAN SUYIN

As a child, my friend Sherrill moved from Atlanta to rural Napa County in California's wine country, which also has many fine dairies. She loved the nature all around her house with the rolling fields and green meadows as her neighbors. One afternoon she brought home another third grader on the school bus and they spent the afternoon in a tree. The two young girls were out exploring in the woods and fields when they lay down under a tree to talk and rest. A group of cows wandered over and surrounded them, or so it seemed to the frightened girls. Up into the tree they scrambled until the cows wandered away. She always felt those cows chased them up the willow and made them stay there. Sherrill spent a lifetime with the fear of cows.

She told me this story as we came to a gate on our walk through Temesal Parkland, and twenty or so cows were parked in front of a gate we needed to proceed through. I showed her how they would be slow but would move away as we walked through them. We both noted that when there is no adult to guide us, we can hold on to old thoughts and fears for a lifetime, and we talked about new beginnings by sharing with a friend. She is my most gentle friend.

Barbara Woodhouse in *Talking to Animals* validates that cows are gentle animals, their tails swishing, chewing on their cuds, their babies standing close: "Talking to animals isn't a matter of words used, it is a matter of your thoughts, your expressions, and above all the tone of your voice. A harsh voice from me can make my cows jump in terror. I shouted at old Queenie once and she got such a shock that she fell down just as if she'd been shot."

Sherril and I take a weekly walk now through an Oakland parkland where the parks allow cows to graze. The path is winding and a bit hilly on one side, and these large, gentle animals stand on the slope just above us watching us pass day after day. In the spring we stop to see the babies feed from the full udders of the mothers. It's a happy time each week, and the gentle cows add to the pleasure of simple yet fulfilling days. And there is no sound of lawn mowers all spring, the grass feeding the animal world until the winter rains come and the sky gods fertilize the earth by rain.

Cows may remind us of our gentler nature. They may remind us of times when we are quite passive. If you look at the cow and see in that animal a sense of delight and wonder, you may find a touchstone or a symbol that helps you know this part of yourself. Sometimes you might describe finding a touchstone as being aware of your body sensations and experiencing a release of feelings. Other times it is a quiet knowing. However it happens, we may be stopped in our tracks and know that we are alive and in alignment with this creature.

The Great Mother, the cow, the symbol of plenty and good, reminds me to slow down. I want to practice maintaining this calm way of being. When I go to North Beach, a bustling Italian area in San Francisco, to meet a friend to write poetry in a café, I sometimes attempt to take mild energy and maintain it no matter what energy the crowds of tourists or the ranting street poets throw my way. Sometimes!

Because the cow is gentle and her udders fill with milk, she is India's sacred cow swollen with life's nourishment. Because she is sacred, she must not be harmed for any reason by anyone. Along with producing milk, it is sometimes said children are the child soul that she produces along with her milk. Her dung is valued because it is used for fuel.

"The cow was one of the most common totemic images of the Great Goddess. The animal herself served as wetnurse to the human race. Cattle were first domesticated in order that people might feed themselves and their children on cow's milk. Thus, the Goddess in India has been the sacred cow, 'fountains of milk and curds,' which meant not only food but also the waters and land masses of earth," explains Barbara G. Walker in *The Woman's Dictionary of Symbols and Sacred Objects*.

Hathor is a cow goddess "who stood in the form of a cow upon the earth in such a way that her four legs were the pillars holding up the sky and her belly was the firmament. Each evening, Horus, as the sun god, flew into her mouth in the form of a hawk and each morning reappeared again reborn. . . . As the cow goddess of Tuat, she was portrayed in Egyptian art wearing a long pendant collar around her neck and the Menait, emblem of joy and pleasure on her back," writes Anthony S. Mercatante in *Who's Who in Egyptian Mythology*.

EXERCISES:

+ Thinking of your spiritual nature, how could more gentleness with the people in your life feed your life?

+ I want grace to walk with me, want to bring it home to you. What do you know about maintaining your energy regardless of what is happening around you? What do you know about joining into energy around you?

20. THE COSMIC EGG *(eggs)*

"In the robin's nest there were Eggs . . . in the garden
there was nothing which did not understand the
wonderfulness of what was happening—the immense, tender,
terrible, heart-breaking beauty and solemnity of Eggs.
If there had been one person in that garden who had not known
through all his or her innermost being that if an Egg were taken
away or hurt the whole world would whirl round and crash
through space and come to an end . . . there could have been
no happiness even in that golden springtime air."

FRANCES HODGSON BURNETT, *THE SECRET GARDEN*

"PUT YOUR EGGS in one basket, and watch the basket," writes Mark Twain, reminding us of trust and the fragility of eggs. Some eggs, such as the egg of the South Pacific bird the megapode, are buried in the sand to be protected and monitored by testing the internal temperature of the nest as the male pulls out beakfulls of sand and uses his tongue as a thermometer. The megapode can then pull off leaves and sand and replace them at night if necessary.

Many eggs are laid in nests high in the glory of a tree; others are laid on the ground in the fields, with the squawking parents nearby to scare you if you come too close to the nest.

We all have pictures in our memory of the chicken pecking its way out of a shell. We see the wet, little thing new with life and can easily appreciate the process. Birth and chickens, eggs and shells, are a part of our childhood that keeps us near origins and reminds us that we take essential nourishment from the offerings of the earth.

At a time of great sadness, I wrote:

One day the broken glass stopped floating
and the world was put back together again.
Time rewound itself to the full egg.

At the time, the images seemed fitting but unusual. Now I see that I must have been subconsciously thinking of trying to put Humpty Dumpty together again, a favorite nursery rhyme of mine. After a loss, the need for something as basic as the egg to be whole.

In Maria Leach's *Folklore, Mythology and Legend*, the egg often represents the earth, life itself, or the seat of the soul. She writes, "In the folklore of most of Europe, the strength of life of supernatural beings could be destroyed only if an egg, usually hidden in the body of one or more animals, in some inaccessible place, was broken. Such separable soul tales have been reported from Italy, Iceland, Ireland, Bohemia, Britany, and Lapland. . . . Eggs also figure prominently in fertility rites, both human and agricultural. In seventeenth century France, a bride upon entering her new home had to break an egg to ensure her fecundity. . . . Eggs are also used in sacrifice, particularly to the dead, and as survivals of tree-worship. The Maori buried their dead with a moa's egg held in one hand; the Khassia of Assam placed an egg in the navel of the corpse."

Eggs mean new beginnings and can be used as a symbol in our journals to begin to feel something new in our soulful journey. We don't have to know how. We don't have to be sure. All we have to do is to write our hope in our journals and ask to find the way.

We have heard of reading tea leaves to forsee the future. Reading an egg is an old custom of healing among European and Native American groups. First, a raw egg, unbroken, was rubbed on the sick person's body. Then, the egg was broken and studied: its appearance revealed the nature of the illness and possible treatments. Chills may require the egg to be heated so the cold taken from the ill person could be transformed. Another way to foretell the future is to drop a raw egg into boiling water and base predictions on shapes that result.

Exercises:

- ◆ Beginnings are times of creation. Where were the beginnings of the awareness of your spiritual life? Write down the events, places, thoughts, people, and ideas that were important at that time.

- ◆ How could you find a place for yourself between the earth and sky?

- ◆ Put a raw egg into boiling water and write what the shapes seem to suggest to your spiritual life.

21. WILD PARAKEETS
OF SAN FRANCISCO *(parakeets)*

> "Wild feathered thing, we hear your echoes in our dreams,
> wake with the pulse of joy hidden in pockets. One day, not so long
> from the first, this heartbeat of freedom will spill over our lives
> like a god, like a spirit, asking us to find a way to fly."
>
> JAN ALICE PFAU

DOLORES AVENUE is a wonderful sloping street winding up and down the hills of the warmest part of San Francisco. The avenue is divided by a grassy center section lined with palm trees. If you lean out of your car window, you'll hear the warble and screeching notes of wild parakeets belting out their songs from the palm trees. Occasionally, along the avenue or in nearby Dolores Park, you can see the parakeets hiding in the thick fronds. A tree may hold as many as fifty nests!

San Franciscans are proud of their long history defending freedom, and because of this value, San Francisco is a city of safe shelter; immigrants will not be deported. Parakeets are now informally considered under the "immigrant umbrella." These parakeets were sold from the forests of South America and were imported into the United States for pets. San Franciscans link the idea of freedom to these birds and love the wild parakeets in their park and trees. The creed of the city and the parakeets fill the imagination with the exotic and with living a life that suits the individual spirit.

This love for parakeets is an example of how we use happenings in our world to create new symbols. Historically, the bird was the messenger from the heavens or was forecasting that something was about to happen. They also are the symbols of the soul and are often used as metaphors in poetry as flying home to the place of peace.

Recently I visited the studio of performance artist Edith Altman. Her live/work studio space is a three-brick-thick warehouse on Chicago's southside. The space is a windowed three stories on the work side and seems high enough to fly to the top of the ivy-covered windows that run to the height of the roof. It was snowing, bringing our attention to the weight of nature on the roof and bringing nature to the city.

I spied a contraption on one of her high shelves and was told by my friend Claire Krantz, who had brought me here, that it was a flying machine. Claire originally met Edith when she came to write an article about her for *Art in America* on flying. On the shelf was Edith's flying gear, a wonderful white suit made of heavy canvas and a spunky hat with tassels. There were photos of Edith wearing her flying suit and coming through a grove of trees preparing to take off. All I really remember is that the suit and the contraption with its twirling oars on its back looked like they could take her on a leap into flight. I left not thinking to ask if it worked. What I cared about was that she wanted to be free and fly.

I know of no story that shows that parakeets help each other escape but Eugene Linden's book, *The Parrot's Lament*, in which he writes, "According to Sally Blanchard, this episode took place in Witchita, Kansas, roughly twenty years ago in a breeding flock of about thirty double yellow-headed parrots. The escape took place while Bill and Wilma Fisher, the couple that raised the parrots, were away at a parrot show. Chango, one of the parrots, used his beak to unscrew the bolts on his cage to the point where it collapsed. Once out, he somehow unlatched the other cages one by one. . . . In the evening, almost all the birds were out and having a parrot party." Perhaps we all need to help each other escape what limits us and find a new symbol for vitality in our lives.

EXERCISES:

◆ Have you ever wanted to fly? What was that fantasy?

◆ How have you flown free from any constraints of your gender, age, race, religion, childhood?

◆ How do you feel about accepting diversity and providing sanctuary for those who do not fit in with the majority?

22. SCENTS OF LIFE *(lavender)*

"People from a planet without flowers would think we must be
mad with joy the whole time to have such things about us."

IRIS MURDOCH

THOSE OF US who write and journal know that some years bring a repeat of subjects and phrases in our writing. One year for me it was the changing forms of love and thickets. More recently it's noticing the joy in the everyday and lavender grasses. Everything I write seems to use the phrase lavender grasses. I've never seen a field of lavender in the French or English countryside but I have this feeling of the purple flame of flower against the silver foliage waving their colors and giving off the heavenly scent of lavender.

If I explore further, I can understand that it is my search for rest and peace that draws me to open fields of grasses and wonderful odors. I remember growing up being lulled by the smells of earth in the meadow next door. This makes fields a personal symbol and reminds me to make a plan to take a day off and kick back and enjoy a day trip to the country or simply rest in my tiny garden. Now lavender plants with their flower looking like fat purple bees grace my rest and act as a symbol to call me to ease.

Beyond my use of a lavender field as a personal symbol, lavender has a history of its own. Because of its sweet but mellow smell, London merchants once sold it as a cure for the plague. Egyptians swaddled mummies in shrouds dipped in lavender as a symbol of peace for the departed.

Perhaps you or a loved one could be reminded of your spirit when you buy something with lavender: lavender soap, lavender bubble bath, lavender oils, lavender shampoo, lavender lotion, lavender plants outside the window where you read or write.

Aromatherapists use lavender for relaxation and many use lavender for sachets and potpourri. (It's easy to dry lavender by hanging it upside down out of sun light. Then as time goes by, strip off the dried flowers.) Why not go about your day noticing the scents in your life? What are you drawn to? If you are not aware of using scents for relaxation, go to a shop that sells fragrant oils or to a nursery or garden and become aware of what you like. Bring this scent into your life to relax or energize your physical body.

EXERCISES:

+ The Hindus give thanks to the five senses by doing rituals with sweet smelling substances at shrines. They might use an ivory scent shaker shaped like a lotus, a symbol of creation, and fill it with a sweet scent. They wave burning incense back and forth in the shrine in an attempt to welcome the gods with sweet smells. What ritual could you set up at your writing time to bring a sweet scent to your spirit and welcome her?

+ Perhaps you could promise to do daily *puja*, as they say in Hinduism, which is to promise to invite your spirit into your life and pray to that spiritual force. What would daily prayer be like for you?

+ Our sense of smell helps us recall memories from our childhood. What scent brings you back to a time that gave joy to your spirit?

23. TASTE OF LIFE *(olive oil)*

> "We live on the leash of our senses."
>
> DIANE ACKERMAN

MOVING TO SAN FRANCISCO, one of the exotic trees I suddenly enjoyed was the olive trees I saw in Golden Gate Park. I was curious about the making of olive oil and read that although there are now machines to help make the oil, much is still done by hand by farmers who have small plots of land. They tumble olives into a huge basin under two large grindstones that crush the olives and seeds. Workers spread the results on mats and stake them on a spindle. A hydraulic press "presses" the crushed olives, and the water and oil slowly drip from the mats into a settling tank. It's in this tank where the oil rises to the top. The oil is then bottled by hand. There is something ancient and "godly" in making olives into oil by hand in the sun-drenched valleys with the geometry of olive vines marching over the hilly fields.

Writing with a pen or pencil on the page is also a holy thing to do. To write with your body, to feel with your heart, to call out with your spirit, and to allow your mind a rest from vigilance, is asking for the soul to look inward and love the life that it holds.

There are many tastes of olive oil, from the rich, fruity, with a peppery aftertaste of classic Tuscan oil, to the soft and sweet Moroccan oil or the pasty bitter oil that the Arabs love. An olive oil connoisseur can tell you what country the olive was grown in and often even the region of that country! It's become a popular sport in San Francisco to know your "oils."

Because the olive tree lives long and its leaves are evergreen, the tree itself is a symbol of longevity and immortality. The calming influence of the oil of the olive makes the olive a symbol of peace. If you dream of gathering olives, it is a symbol of delightful surprises to come! To eat them in your dreams signifies faithful friends and contentment.

Chevalier and Gheerbrant's *Dictionary of Symbols* explains that "the olive is a symbol of peace and it was an olive-branch which the dove brought back to Noah when the Flood was over. An old legend tells that Christ's cross was made of olive- and cedar-wood. In medieval terms, it was, furthermore, a symbol of gold and of love. 'Were I to behold olive-wood gilded at your door, I would at once call you a temple of God,' Angeles wrote, fired by a description of Solomon's Temple."

Next time you dunk bread into olive oil or cook with it, I hope you will remember some of this history and enjoy the flavor presented to you from the olive and the sacred oil tree. The oil from nature can be one more connection to the earth.

EXERCISES:

+ Make a habit to try a few new foods every month. Put basil in your salad if you usually don't. Add rosemary to your chicken. Foods and herbs new to you can nourish your sense of spirit in addition to nourishing your body. What would you like to try and what holds you back from trying new tastes?

+ What new foods and herbs have you brought into your life for which you have "a taste"?

24. A CUP OF TEA *(tea)*

"Tea quenches tears and thirst."

JEANINE LARMOTH AND CHARLOTTE TURGEON

SO MANY OF US, when we are in turmoil, sit down for a minute with a good, hot cup of tea. Author Alice Walker writes, "Tea to the English is really a picnic indoors." Ayn Rand, the author and philosopher, once said, "After the English Empire collapses, two things will remain: the tea ritual and mystery novels."

Tea is a time when we often do a bit of a ritual, even if we don't notice that we do. It may not be as elaborate as a Japanese tea ceremony, but we choose one of our favorite tastes, steep it as weak or as strong as we like, add sugar, honey, or milk, and relax. We go through the motions knowing we are heading toward comfort. It may symbolize our human need to care for ourselves within the hours of our day.

A neighbor from Japan told me that the Japanese tea ceremony is a gateway to feeling our spiritual self. Tea is taken in the *roji* (garden) where there is *chahitsu* (tea house). The tea is sipped slowly and enjoyed in a state of inner composure. In this state, you are to concentrate on inner and outer harmonies, your breath, the sight of the garden, the beauty of the simple cups, enjoyment of the weather. The feeling of this experience should then extend to the rest of your day.

"In Zen Buddhism, [tea is a] ceremonial drink associated with intense meditation, a symbolism supported by a Japanese legend that the first tea plant grew from the eyelids of the Bodhidharma who cut them off to stay awake. Qualities emphasized in the etiquette of the tea ceremony are purity, harmony, tranquility and the beauty of simplicity," writes Jack Tresidder in his *Dictionary of Symbols*.

In Central Asia, teahouses serve as community gathering places. Friends gather to share the day's events or to tell the family news over a cup of tea. When I was in Colorado for my son's wedding, I happened on The Boulder Dushanbe Teahouse where they served eighty varieties of loose leaf teas. The Teahouse was a gift from the people of Dushanbe, in the area once known as the Persian Empire situated south of the Silk Road trails. The teahouse in Boulder is a replica of their ancient teahouse and reflects Persian decoration of the heavens, the sun, and flowers on lavishly colored tiles. The designs date back nearly 2,000 years, and it is the perfect setting to relax and feel your spirit. Why not find a place near where you live or work that makes a good cup of tea in a pretty setting? Special places freely chosen are a way of loving yourself.

My friend Suzanne gave me a tiny tea pot with matching cups, a tray to serve my tea on, and a red silk square cloth. I loved this birthday gift, which I saw as a reminder to relax and pay attention. I was especially touched by the loving detail of the silk cloth. Using such material as a napkin or placing it on the tray under the tea pot, I could not help notice its beauty and feel part of history. Each time I use it, I am going out of my way to care for myself. An everyday ritual, a wake-up call that says I am spirit.

I had a client with a reccurring tea dream in which she was thirsty for tea. In interpreting this part of the dream together, we felt it symbolized surprise because after this thirst something unexpected happened, such as uninvited visitors or a trip to see someone long gone from her life.

Merce Cunningham, the famous dancer and choreographer, had a policy whereby the dance, the music, the set, and the costumes were worked out independently and then brought together as a piece. The pieces showed the magic in chance; the dances were weird and awkward and strangely alive. Cunningham helps us rethink development as something other than simply a step-by-step process. He shows us that although traditional tea serving and ceremonies are beautiful in their precision, strange shapings and unusual movements can also be wonderfully appealing. For instance, try reading the tea leaves at the bottom of your cup. Note the shape and design. What beauty and message can you see in this random organization that might help your spirit?

EXERCISES:

◆ Read the tea leaves at the bottom of a cup of tea. Ask what the spirit can tell you about work, friendship, your body, love.

◆ Using the tea for refreshment and then allowing messages to come from the tea leaves reminds me of our writing process. All is needed: the healing of the drink, the message, the warming of words, again, the message. When making cognac, the first vapors are distilled off, which the French call, *part des anges*, an offering. Write about how often the first part of what you write is an offering for the angels.

◆ How do you feel about rituals? Do you have some in your life? Perhaps there is a ceremony you could do for yourself using tea. Remember the tea comes from the wise earth. It was once a growing thing and now it is offered to you to soothe or refresh you. Do you need a tray or a special pot or cup? You might choose a special place near a window to sip your tea, remembering your creative spirit lives.

25. RATTLES AND COILS *(snakes)*

"Have you ever studied a snake's face?
How optimistic they look. They have an eternal smile."

TASHA TUDOR

I HAVE A FRIEND who says every time she goes on vacation, she first has to pass the place of her fear by encountering a snake. In northeast Arizona while visiting the ancient cliff dwellers, she crossed a river with snakes swimming near the boat. In Egypt, a cobra almost bit her. Last year, she told me, she almost stepped on a five-foot western garden snake with his yellow-ribboned streaks. A brown mottled gopher snake slid by her on her first hike through a field of grass in Michigan. After arriving at the Zen retreat in Santa Cruz, California, on a hot August afternoon, she went swimming at the waterhole and felt a water snake slither over her legs. She says snakes signal her to wake up and be aware of nature's promise and danger.

The fear and repulsion of snakes is common; the snake is known to be associated with so-called baser human instincts that keep us tied to lower consciousness and keep us away from our spiritual path. The Grecian myth of Medusa, with snakes in her hair, was a goddess changed into a harridan who could turn men into stone with her gaze. Medusa symbolized the fear of men toward woman, particularly of their feelings.

To the Buddhists, the green snake is a symbol for hatred, which keeps Buddha away from a person on the way to enlightenment. Sometimes snakes are used as fetishes for regeneration, wisdom, wholeness, good fortune, and rain. Other times they are fetishes for transformation and shrewdness.

Maria Leach's *Folklore, Mythology and Legend* teaches us that in ancient Hopi symbolism "the snakes have rain-bringing power, and are also venerated as legendary ancestors. These 'elder brothers' are descended from a snake hero who married a snake maiden after a long voyage, and brought forth a progeny of snakes." Well in advance of the ceremonial prayer for rain, "the medicine men gather snakes and wash them in yucca suds for purification. They gather bull snakes, whip snakes, and rattle snakes. During the secret kiva rituals the young people of the Snake and Antelope societies join in ceremonial races" with the finale being the release of the snakes to the four directions to go on their mission to find rain.

Perhaps you have been lucky enough to find a discarded skin of a snake. The molting is done by the snake finding a rough hard object and rubbing its nose and chin against it until its skin breaks. Once the head is freed, the snake wriggles its body until the whole skin peels off, inside out. A new layer of skin forms beneath the old one before this molting takes place. How often in our lives do we feel that we have changed, shed our skin, and wish there was a sign to the people in our lives that says, "New me. New me." That's when the spirit keeps us company until we catch up with ourselves.

At birth a rattlesnake has a bulbous swelling at the tip of its tail. The tail end of its old skin cannot be pulled over this swelling; thus, it forms a beginning of a rattle. As successive molts take place, the tip of the skin that cannot be shed forms a ring around a bone known as the shaker, made up of the last seven or eight vertebrae, which fuse together soon after the snake is born. We don't know what the rattle is used for, a warning to others, a way of starling prey. We do know that you can tell the age of a rattlesnake by allowing one year for every two rings. If the snake is a scary reptile for you, think about it's ability to warn people of its presence. Think about how you could change the symbol of snake linked with fear to the part of you that warns, moves, and changes.

There's an interesting little book, *Muir Among the Animals*, in which naturalist John Muir writes of his experiences with wildlife. In his story about snakes he writes, "Small fellow mortals, gentle and guileless, they are easily tamed, and have beautiful eyes, expressing the clearest innocence, so that, in spite of prejudices brought from cool, lizardless countries, one must soon learn to like them. . . . Most of them glint and dart on the sunny rocks and across open spaces from bush to bush, swift as dragonflies and humming-birds, and about as brilliantly colored. . . . If you stay with them a week or two and behave well, these gentle saurians, descendants of an ancient race of giants, will soon know and trust you, come to your feet, play, and watch your every motion with cunning curiosity."

When you dream about a snake, it can have many different interpretations, depending on the context of the snake in the dream. Basically, the snake symbolizes a primitive form of animal life, and therefore a deep layer of the unconscious. To dream that a snake coils itself around you with its tongue darting at you may be a symbol of feeling powerless in the hands of others. To step on a snake in a dream is often a symbol of troubles coming and to see a snake bite another fortells that some friend will be hurt or criticized by you.

Linda Hogan, a writer from the Chickasaw tribe, tells the positive meaning of snake in the old days. "Before Snake became the dark god of our underworld, burdened with human sin, it carried a different weight in our human bones; it was a being of holy inner earth. The smooth gold eye, the hundred ribs holding life, it coiled beautifully and mysteriously around the world of human imagination. In nearly all ancient cultures the snake was the symbol of healing and wholeness. Even the old ones, like the Adena people, who left no recorded history, left a tribute to the snake in one of the mounds near Chillicothe, Ohio. Over 1,200 feet in length, the mound is an earth sculpture of an open-mouthed serpent that clasps an egg, a new potential for life, between its jaws. This is only one of many worldwide images of snakes, some curling about an egg, others with tail in mouth, telling us about the germinal beginnings of life and renewal, of infinity gone in a circle round itself."

EXERCISES:

+ When you think of the circle of a snake's coil and its connection to totality, how are you becoming more whole?

+ Are there times when you protected yourself when it was unnecessary and even drove someone away? Are there times when you could have been more careful and gotten to know a person better before being open with them? What does your spirit say is the difference, and what have you learned?

✦ Do you ever feel you are speeding somewhere fast and somewhere undetermined? What is that feeling for you?

26. THE MOON, THAT PEARL *(moon)*

"The moon is a fish that swims underwater in the daytime."
BARBARA BROOKS

THE MOON sits in the sky waning or waxing, asking us to notice her in changing shape and luminous eye. The beauty in the waxing and waning moon is a reminder that change and constancy are something to count on.

In the crescent moon, I have felt the power of the newborn. I have seen the new moon holding the old moon in her arms and felt my imagination fed by that sight. I read that once the crescent moon symbolized the ship of light that carries the soul through the darkness and into the light of the new dawn. I have watched the wax of light disappear, black clouds covering the moon, the red sun eaten.

The moon begs for poetry. I wrote this for a dear friend, Suzanne. It says in part:

I have waited for this full moon that now sits in my hands . . . .
Sometimes I feel I'm joining life again and there isn't anything that
    doesn't shine: yellow, the crème, the purple glaze
of wild iris. These are the times I am attracted to round things: a bowl of
    apples, a woman's breast, at the bottom of a vase, pebbles anchoring home.

The last stanza of a Joan Annsfire poem reads:

The moon rises round and polished silver,
a merciful beacon bright as her feathers.
A rose and orange sunset fades to gray

as she rises into the evening,
a lost emissary, an indigo shadow,
a dream of green water.

See what you have up your folded sleeve to say about the moon outside your window.

The full moon echoes meanings of the circle, which signifies wholeness. We often hear the saying *to come full circle*. The waxing moon for the peoples of European cultures was the best time to plant seeds because the waxing moon held fertility. Have you ever entered your bedroom and sat watching reflections, the moon and the mirror? Look at the moon and think of these symbols and stories and feel what the moon might do for you tonight.

I have seen moonlight that looked like a fall of snow. I have sat under the moon and felt myself enveloped in its power of healing. Start to record your different experiences with the moon. You may be surprised how often the moon has a spiritual reminder for you. I can be lost in the everyday and look up to see a reminder in the moon's roundness that I don't *have* a soul, I *am* a soul. I can feel a tiredness in my bones that seems impossible to cure and see in the moon that true rest lies just a thought away.

I decided to choose a name for myself when I became single in my mid-thirties. I had thought about many names and one night I dreamed about my favorite aunt, Nell, and the moon peeking over the hill of her home. Nell stayed up late reading and watching the changing moon. The moon reminded me of Nell and my father's side of the family. I woke up, added *ell* from Nell to my birth name, Jan, and gave myself the moon. Now I was Janell Moon.

This naming story reminds me of the face of God I see when I am praying. I had to reconcile the traditional images of God with my own experience. I wanted a more feminine, loving presence in my god. I use the moon, whose face I cannot see but is everywhere with me as I pray. It is important for you to think and write about how you envision spirit. There is no right or wrong way, but there is your way.

I also liked knowing that the moon's rock was bluish and crystalline in some areas and green with the familiar air pockets in others. I thought of how the moon has its own various rocks shaped by the processes that have sculpted its surface. We too are shaped by the family and cultural processes with which we are asked to live. Our environment determines the colors of our flag in many ways. The moon reflects us in many ways.

The American Indians used sign language so when two tribes met on the trail they could communicate with each other. Because they lived so closely to the earth and its moon, the sign for moon was the sign of *night* (hands folded across chest with right arm resting on top of left) and then a crescent moon shape with forefinger and thumb. Their calendar reckoned months by the moon, which waxes and wanes every twenty-eight days. Therefore, they lived by thirteen months a year. The signs of the month were named by descriptions such as January, the snow moon, April, the green grass moon, and July, the thunder moon.

Perhaps no other natural object has been more linked to women than the moon. Because of its connection with women's menstruation cycle, the moon became a symbol of Mother Goddess everywhere. It is linked with the power of the dark, mysterious side of nature. We can love the moon and the dark, mysterious side of ourselves.

In *The Fountainhead*, Ayn Rand writes, "He wondered whether the peculiar solemnity of looking at the sky comes, not from what one contemplates, but from that uplift of one's head." And the moon too. We remember to lift our head to the sky and suddenly see the moon hanging there, over the trees, from hill to hill, like a ball of gleaming wax, waiting—asking for us.

EXERCISES:

✦ The moon is an outline of your own experience. When you see the full moon what do you see? Crescent moon? A sliver of the moon?

✦ When you are dreaming, the moon climbs the sky. What does it take to change a moment into holiness?

✦ The moon goddess was almost universally understood as the weaver of fate and the controller of destinies, in the same way, she controlled the tides, the weather, rainfall, and the seasons. Write about the dark, mysterious side of your nature and how fate has controlled part of your life.

27. ALWAYS, AND AGAIN *(dawn)*

"Nothing, of course, begins at the time you think it did."
                                            LILLIAN HELLMAN

WHEN I WAS YOUNGER, I never liked to see the dawn unless I was still up. I wanted my sleep. Now I'll get up just to feel my spirit and to have the solitude that dawn offers. I remember a quote from writer Bessie Head that always made me laugh: "So sudden and abrupt was the sunrise that the birds had to pretend they had been awake all the time."

The dawn was the rebirth of the day and that for which spirits of ancient cultures sacrificed themselves in order to nourish the day and the sun. The dawn is always young. The dawn is like a child wet from birth, its dew shining in mother's hand. When the sun rises, "That is always such a forgiving time. When that first cold, bright streak comes over the water, it's as if all our sins were pardoned; as if the sky leaned over the earth and kissed it and gave it absolution," writes Willa Cather.

Dawn reminds us of second chances. A close friend once told me it took her three times to be emotionally solid enough to stand by a dying friend. The first two times she was faced with a loved one's death, she felt herself retreat emotionally, and sometimes physically, to protect herself. But then she finally got it right. Years later when she became ill and after her subsequent death, I found myself at her memorial repeating what she had told me. I talked about second chances and how the birds in their nests of hair and grasses want to help us fly to a place beyond the dry mosses *duras penas*, through hard pain.

I saw many grateful faces; her death had been particularly hard, and I realized I wasn't alone in a feeling of disappointment with myself. I was able to say that her ending was not her life; her life had been filled with song and taffy. (It's interesting that when we say our hard truth it's often helpful for others.) I gradually forgave myself for all I couldn't do and promised to try to do better at the next dawn. It's what she would have wanted. If you have a place in you that needs this kind of forgiveness, I hope my encouragement might help you do this for yourself. If so, write a prayer for forgiveness and let the next dawn make it so. We all need more mercy for ourselves.

I recently saw the movie *First and Main* directed by David Mamet. It was the story of second chances being more than having another chance to do the wrong thing. The writer in the movie was finding his way to truth in the harsh realities of film making. I found it amusing as I watched him manage to cross a field full of land mines (people in the industry) intact. He found a way to live with his integrity and still write. He had used his awareness as a new dawn of beginnings.

When I'm up at dawn I see the world in which I live in a different light. The white breath of dew covering the grass, a mist over the bay, plants and life seeming so still and fresh. I think of lines from a poem I wrote:

I want the dawn to come gentle,
no wrinkle in the day,
the clock turned toward seven,
raccoons retreating into the dark bellies
of houses, the ground ready
for sprouting: a woman starting her day
holding a spade, a spoon, a pen.

Dawn helps us put our lives in perspective. We are given dawn when mystery seems to be what's true, and that is okay. We are given a dawn to see that we are but a small part of the mystery of the world. Katherine was traveling in Asia and spent an afternoon with an Asian couple she met as she wandered around. She asked them why in Asian paintings and photographs the people were so small. They looked surprised and hesitated, and she realized they probably didn't know much about art and maybe she had made them feel awkward. However, the women raised her hand as if to gesture, "Wait a minute, I'm thinking." Then she carefully said, "Nature so big, people so small," and looked pleased with her correct answer. They all laughed, and this seen truth made a good connection between them.

I thought of the history of photography. Photographs were first used to document a situation, and I considered how scale was used in the 1860s photographs of Yosemite: spectacular trees and mountain peaks with tiny, tiny objects called people at their feet. There were photographs of dawn raising its head, showing its eyes, leaving behind the deep shadows of darkness. And a teeny person watching splendor happen. Through the years people have grown in size in photography. Perhaps there is a metaphor here of valuing the earth as much as we do ourselves. We need to pray that the dawn will always be waiting for us, to make sure we will see a crack of light, and then another, and then loved ones in the light of dawn.

Dawn reminds us that our lives can be more than our dreams in black and white, that there is so much life beyond who we thought we were and what we thought was possible. And we don't have to plan new things but only to continue writing our lives, a ladder with hands and feet to the spirit.

To Buddhists the dawn is the time of enlightenment. To the Greeks it is a time of happiness and beginnings. To the Islamic, the dawn is the state of fresh beginnings and awareness. To watch the dawn in a dream is to know that an opening is happening within you, more awareness, more forgiveness, less resentment.

Dawn is a writer's muse. Homer in the *Odyssey* says, "As soon as Dawn with her rose-tinted hands had lit the East . . ." Or Richard Henry Horne's, "Tis always morning somewhere in the world." Three hundred years ago Saint Theresa said, "Words lead to deeds. . . . They prepare the soul, make it ready and move it toward tenderness."

EXERCISES:

+ Write a prayer that asks for what you would be willing to do. An example might be a prayer for care of the earth, and then be willing to pick up litter on your next hike.

✦ Let yourself break your routine to feel once again connected to the creation of a day. Why not wake at dawn and write a poem to describe the dawn in you?

✦ Dawn is a change to count on. How can your spirit give you second chances?

28. WHERE HOPE LIVES *(stars)*

> "We walk up the beach under the stars.
> And when we are tired of walking,
> we lie flat on the sand under a bowl of stars.
> We feel stretched, expanded to take in their compass.
> They pour into us until we are filled with stars, up to the brim."
>
> ANNE MORROW LINDBERGH

WISHING ON A STAR is not a foolish thing to do! It may be an imaginative child's hope pinning wishes on the first evening star. Or, a woman after years of service wanting to reach for her own stars. Star wishing sometimes helps us follow our hidden loves and unfinished youthful promises.

Katherine Mansfield talks about her connection to solace from the stars: "I love the evening star. Does that seem foolish? I used to go into the backyard, after sunset, and wait until it shone above the dark gum tree. I used to whisper, 'There you are my darling.' And just that first moment it seemed to be shining for me alone."

When my son was traveling around Asia with a backpack, I would gaze at the stars, remember that these same stars shone on him, and wish him safety. Sometimes I would go to the ocean and watch the stars in their brilliance. I would feel connected to him. I was also reminded of the magnificence of all things, and it would put my concerns in perspective.

Maria Leach writes in *Folklore, Mythology and Legend* that "among the Skidi Pawnee the morning and evening stars represented the masculine and feminine elements, and were connected with the advent and the perpetuation on earth of all living forms. Among the Fox Indians, some of the stars are great and powerful spirits; most of them are people who have died and gone to live in the sky. . . . Among the spirits the stars are given a rather prominent place and referred to as 'grandfathers'; they are thought to render service in that they help illuminate the world at night. . . . The Pueblo and other Southwestern Indians also accord the stars prominence as spirits: the Morning Star (often called the Big Star), the Evening Star, the Pleiades, Orion and the Galaxy."

"Tales of humans and animals being caught up into the sky to become a constellation are widespread in Native American, African, Asian, and European lore. One common Native American tale tells how a human girl falls in love with the stars and shuns a human husband; she is taken up to the sky and marries a star. . . . Her son survives to become a great hero. Many culture heroes are said to enter the sky as constellations rather than die," writes Alison Jones in *Dictionary of World Folklore.*

She goes on to write: "A particularly interesting variation in star-gazing is found in Australia, where above the deserts the clear skies appear packed with stars. The Aborigines like most cultures projected pictures such as the figure of the emu onto the night sky, but they tended to use for these the gaps between the stars, the 'dark constellation,' a sort of negative to the usual approach."

The Star of David is part of Jewish mysticism and is made up of two triangles, the upward-pointing being the sun, fire, and male energy, the downward-pointing the moon, water, and female energy. The two triangles balance and make the star.

I have found that there are months when I don't notice the stars, and then, one night they are my delight. I have promised and promised again to stay aware and watch these hearts of fire. I have asked myself what if stars were only out one night a year, what would that celebration be? Famous photographer Edward Weston made a note in his daybook that he was back photographing nature and now seeing the world with different eyes. It happens to all of us: this forgetting our jeweled sky and something then happens and we are blinded well again.

Just being aware. To wake up to what we are given. "Pegasus and Andromeda faced me brilliantly when I lifted my shade, so I went down and had a friendly reunion with the constellations. . . . I get a wonderful peace and the most exquisite pleasure from my friendship with the stars," says writer Ellen Glasgow. After writing this I feel life is remembering and forgetting, coming back to life and the earth.

I like the belief that stars hold tiny souls waiting to become born. The ancients generally regarded the stars as alive: sometimes heavenly angels, sometimes great heroes, others times the souls of the living or dead.

Shooting stars bring much to the imagination. We often make a wish or consider it lucky just to have seen the shooting star. In ancient China a shooting star marked the birth of a child, whose soul was coming to us at that moment. Because the stars' place is in the sky (or heavens as religious traditions believe), they are high above us, with the sacred. It is a place that asks us to lift our heads up to and examine the life of our spirit.

EXERCISES:

+ Do stars twinkle because we blink or believe?

+ In ancient China the stars played a major role on New Year's Day when everyone offered a sacrifice to "his" or "her" star. Choose a star tonight and write what you need to give up to feel your spirit a bit more. Make a commitment tonight on "your" star to be willing to do that. Write about your willingness until it is strong enough to do it.

+ There are many designs on blankets and vases that use stars and the starry sky. Consider nature's influence on art and architecture as you look for decorative motifs taken from nature. Or check out an art museum and see how nature inspired paintings and drawings.

+ If you were going to say a one-sentence prayer three times a day, what would it be? Write it down and carry it with you so you remember. Do this as a practice for a month. Write it in a silver prayer book. Next month, choose another prayer and say twelve prayers in the next twelve months.

29. THE PLENTIFUL SKY (sky)

> "Terrestrial scenery is much, but it is not all.
> Men go in search of it; but the celestial scenery
> journeys to them; it goes its way round the world.
> It has no nation; it costs no weariness, it knows no bonds."
>
> ALICE MEYNELL

I AM ALWAYS IMPRESSED when I go to the islands of Hawaii how large the sky appears. I feel its solemn and majestic presence, and I sit in its awe and pray with open eyes. The expanse reminds me of what Dodi Smith wrote in *I Capture the Castle*: "Flat country seems to give the sky such a chance." This miracle sky, during these times, gives me the chance to lift my head and step out into the blaze of possibility. It's the spirit nearby, showing off her dazzling outfit of hope.

I was restless last night and so I sat down and started reading poetry. I came upon a small accordion-folded chapbook by Howard Hart that City Lights published. In a poem he talked about how the whole sky is needed for the flight of one butterfly. It reminded me of Alan Watts's idea of how everything is needed just as it is to make whatever is happening at the moment happen. Look at the sky and note how it is. Now look at the ferns blowing or hear a bird chirping or watch people passing by, perhaps a horn beeping. All of this makes this moment, and you, by reading these words on this page, are part of it, and you make this moment be as it is.

In Jewish ritual there is an underlying design to help Jews reflect and be sensitive to the small moments in life. "Shabbat begins eighteen minutes before sundown, and ends when three stars have appeared in the sky. Traditional Jews are thus keenly aware of the yearly patterns of sunset, coming earlier in the winter and then later toward summer. Rosh Hodesh, the beginning of the Jewish month, is tied to the appearance of the moon (now calculated mathematically). Some feminists have even suggested that the custom of a woman's going to a *mikveh* (a ritual bath) after the conclusion of her menstrual period has the capacity to evoke an awareness of nature, of the miraculous functioning of a woman's body, and of a deep spiritual quality," writes Daniel Gordis in *God Was Not in the Fire*.

Start to notice the heavens in your everyday life. Perhaps you have a memory of a work of art where the artist used clouds as the halo around the heads of saints and heroes. Watch the blue of the sky changing and the colors of a sunset displaying its ribbons. Enjoy the sky as the roof provided for you. No matter where you are, begin to remember to look up.

A trip to a planetarium may help you discover the "dome-ness" or roundness of our world. That's what it did for a friend. It made her wonder where she had been all her life that she hadn't realized that the world was sculptural. She saw that limitations can be accepted as the truth! As she leaned back in her chair in the dark, she viewed Rochester, New York, from the center so the edges of the city were seen. The city was projected in the round, and the clouds were all around. On the way to a lecture the next day, she saw exactly the same thing.

All her life she had framed things like a photograph, a rectangle in front of her. Now she noticed that clouds at the horizon go up and up and then around and down to the horizon behind us. It was like knowing her belly was part of her back or knowing that what is behind her is still part of what is going on, what is being seen. As I drove back home from talking to her, I looked in the rearview mirror for safety and thought, "Yes, the frame of what is happening is in front of me and in back of me."

For ancient peoples, the skies were the holders of spiritual needs. The sun and rain allowed life to continue growing. The moon held the power of the mystery. The stars held tales of bears and giants. In most cultures, the rising sun at dawn is a symbol of hope and new beginning.

In Celtic traditions, there is no difference between sky or heavens. They regarded the heavens as a vault, and feared that the sky would fall upon their heads. The Iroquois believe that humans came from the sky and came to earth when Sky Woman fell through a hole. The earth animals quickly spread out the earth on the back of a turtle to provide a home for her.

We learn from J. C. Cooper's *Illustrated Encyclopaedia of Traditional Symbols* that the sky is "transcendence; infinity, height; the Heavens; the realm of bliss; sovereignty; order in the universe. Sky gods are usually creators, omnipotent and omniscient, and symbolize cosmic rhythms. They are guardians of the law; Under a matriarchy, sky deities are usually feminine, occasionally the sky divinity is asexual. In Hindu symbolism the sky is the sieve, through which the *soma* juice is forced, falling as rain, fertilizing the land and accompanied by thunder and lightning."

A friend lived in a white house on a hill with so much grass around it looked like a park. It was a sloping lawn with a down off to the edge of the beach. The sky was clear by the water because the atmosphere doesn't get reflected light from the city. On balmy nights, she would lie down on the grass and take in the silence and watch the northern lights. No light show could ever reproduce what it was like, she said. It wasn't like field painting which is continuous texture without focus. It was dense in its collections of light, sparkling pinpoints of light. The whole thing was moving, starting at the horizon, like a ceiling of light. It was like the goddess of the world wanting to be noticed as she spread out her jewels.

EXERCISES:

+ Imagine the sky as particles touching the top of your head, asking you to be here with it. How could you accept this day, this time of your life?

+ If the sky holds the light for humans to see by, how could it also hold honesty for you to live by? What would your life be like if you were really honest with yourself?

+ Write a poem of utter contentment under the roof of the sky. (If you don't have an experience, promise yourself to make time this weekend and give yourself a few hours of bliss.) Maybe use the line of *hopping kangaroos*. Here's an example:

At the Spa

The hum of language I don't recognize
helps me rest, my stomach yawning
an O under a pile of papers
sliding onto the cement
as I slip to sleep
under the arbor of wisteria.
I am the Queen of Heart and I can have anything,
cheeses wrapped in a leaf,
fresh lemonade from a cart stand,
stacks of pink terry cloth towels.
The fronds of palms wave their raveling,
the sky blue, clear of hopping kangaroos.

30. A STRING OF SEA SHELLS *(shells)*

> "Three things needed are a book, a clock, a shell:
> wisdom, the heart, and the imagination."
>
> JUDY KANE

THE NECKLACE SHELL holds a small being that is a settler on the sands. It lays its eggs in coiled, straplike bands, a shape suitable for stringing. It is a common predator that plows through the sand in search of food. It drills holes in bivalve shells and eats the animals inside. Not as dainty a picture as you might assume from its name!

To wander by the sea collecting sea shells has been solace to many who are going through change or are searching for their way. The San Francisco Pacific Ocean beaches offer many shells, among them the sand dollar. It is round and bleached-white-looking and holds the image of a five-petal blossom on the top and a poinsettia-like pattern on the underside. The sand dollar is actually a sea urchin that has adapted to life on warm, sandy shores. They have tiny spines and a flattened shape that improves their stability on the sea bed, showing us once again how nature takes care of its own. To find a sand dollar, so beautiful and well formed, is to be given an offering of nature; it can be used, much like a stone, as a reminder that the natural world saves you.

Shells that can be found on the shore help us to use our "close-looking." At low tide the beach looks barren, but a close inspection will reveal evidence in the shapes of a variety of holes and tracks that give evidence that animals have dug down to where they can find moisture. Sometimes hundreds of shells can be living right where you are walking, such as the sundial, spotted diggers, masked crab, razor shell, and sand and tusk shells.

Well known for its smooth, glossy, colorful shell is the cowrie. "Cowries were used by early man as a form of exchange. Most frequently used was the inch-long, yellow Money Cowrie of the Indian and western Pacific oceans. It has been found in the burial grounds of North American Indians, evidently brought to this continent by earlier fur traders as a trade item. The most valuable cowries came from the tropical waters of the southwestern Pacific," write Old and Emerson in their Golden Field Guide, *Seashells of North America*.

The flat, dishlike abalone shell is well known for its iridescent beauty and use as a favorite food. Old and Emerson continue: "Indians of the southwestern Pacific used abalones as ornaments and utensils. Numerous trade routes from California to southwestern and central United States have been traced by means of shell remains in ancient burial sites."

In *Folklore, Mythology, and Legend*, Maria Leach says, "Shells share water's symbolic association and are linked to the moon and to the feminine, yin principle. Venus, goddess of love, was born in the waters and transported to land on a scallop shell. In China shells symbolize a successful journey and good fortune, and in Christianity they represent the baptismal waters perhaps because shells were sometimes used to carry water. Those shells that consist of two halves fused together are symbolic of secrecy or sexual passion, and shellfish such as oysters are thought to be aphrodisiacs."

I had a client who repeatedly dreamed of gathering shells. To her, it meant gathering extravagance. Depending on the context of the dream, this was either positive or negative. Once, she dreamed of gathering shells and then finding herself in a grove of fir surrounding a stone circle. There was a fire, and people were chanting; she felt safe and welcomed to a home she had never seen but knew as familiar. She walked through the people and gave the shells to the altar of the fire. A spiritual gift and a homecoming. Another time, she gathered shells and found herself in a factory of steel things. It was beautiful but strange to be in a place of shining metal reality. She was curious and wandered around. Everything in the factory was hers, but she had no key to start anything; nothing could be used. She searched and searched for the key and never found it. She felt frustrated after dreaming this dream. After talking about it, she realized that, although beautiful in its own way, there was nothing there she wanted or needed.

I keep a basket of shells on my dining room table because they are beautiful and are a reminder of the ocean. Every so often I add a shell I have found, and it brings the memory back to me a while longer. I send loved ones in Illinois and Ohio shells as a reminder of me and as an echo of the sea: remember me, remember me. Personal symbols, shells have an ancient living history.

What a pleasure it is to bring a conch shell to our ear and hear "the sound of the ocean." I could tell you the conch shell intensifies the sounds it picks up from its spiral interior, which brings the "sound of the ocean," but that wouldn't satisfy the magical part of us that believes a tiny part of the ocean lives in the womb of the conch shell. Listen again; it's the ocean reminding you of the Mother, the salt air, and the chant of waves.

EXERCISES:

+ The quotation at the beginning of this section uses dream symbolism of the book, clock, and shell. In what areas of your life do all three come into play? Explore this idea.

+ How could you use a shell as a personal symbol?

31. FINDING MORE *(thistles)*

> "Nemo me impune lacessit" (None touches me unharmed).
>
> SCOTTISH SAYING

THISTLES have deeply indented leaves tipped with sharp prickles and can be found standing two to five feet high in fields, meadows, and vacant lots. Flowers originate from the burrlike structures. Thistles symbolize prickliness and the possibility of vengeance.

The best memories one of my clients had were of outdoor play in the fields around her house in Richmond, California. She tells of a field of grass at the dead end at the top of Roosevelt Avenue on Ventura that was so high and green that she and her friends would get down on their knees and make tunnels. Their only difficulty was when they ran into a thistle, for the spikes hurt. She recalls returning to school when the field turned brown and the thistles were but skeletons.

The thistle is an example in nature showing that what can hurt you can also feed you. The "sow's thistle" is so named because pigs eagerly consume the plant. The stem may be cooked as greens and the roots eaten boiled or roasted. The sap of the sow's thistle is used to fight opium addiction.

My sister and I used to often take a drive to the countryside outside of Akron, Ohio, on Sundays, when my nephew was young. We enjoyed stopping at the roadside stands for tomatoes and corn and pausing at the lovely open spaces. We would put on gloves and cut thistles to make a dried-flower autumn bouquet. These memories make a personal symbol mwhich is probably how thistles got a chapter of their own in this book.

Thistles also symbolize protectiveness. They are the national emblem of Scotland because of a tradition that tells of a raiding party of Danes heard screaming, giving themselves away, as they crept up to the tenth-century Staines Castle in the dark. The moat was dry and full of thistles.

Barbara Walker writes in *The Woman's Dictionary of Symbols and Sacred Objects*, "The thistle was declared symbolic of original sin, because of the biblical passage about God's curse on the land: 'Cursed is the ground for thy sake. . . . Thorns also and thistles shall it bring forth to thee' (Genesis 3:17-18). . . . Some medieval herbalists believed that thistles could cure melancholia and plague. The 'caroline thistle' was named after Charlemagne because of a certain legend: Charlemagne, on God's instructions, shot an arrow into the air to find a cure for such diseases as melancholia and plague, and it landed on that particular kind of thistle, God's own revelation of a cure."

In ancient times it was believed that thistles could help keep away evil powers if hung on your front door. In the Christian tradition the thistle is used as a symbol for Christ's suffering. Because thistles do not lose their form, the Chinese use thistles as a symbol for loyalty.

Thistles are also a personal symbol because of the memory of my father reading *Winnie the Pooh* to my sister and me. If I remember it correctly after forty-some years, it was Eyore the donkey who didn't know what he liked to eat, and his animal friends tried to help him find out. Finally they discovered he liked thistles! I remember laughing out loud just thinking that a donkey would like to eat thistles. It really doesn't matter if I don't remember the story exactly. What matters is that when I see thistles, I remember my father and sister before being tucked in for the night in that four-poster bed.

EXERCISES:

✦ If you live anywhere near a countryside, take a trip and make a day for yourself creating symbols of relaxation. Write in your journal your own personal symbols and what they mean to you. I might jot down what I told you about thistles. I might write *berries* and how beauty means gratitude (gifts from nature) for me. I would write about *space* and the ease it gives me to imagine and dream. Start today with symbols you may already have from vacations, holidays, days off, or fond memories. Expand your list over time by taking day trips. Be aware that you can create personal meaning from elements of nature.

✦ What does your Buddha nature know about the idea that what can hurt you can also feed you?
✦ List some personal symbols of your own and what memory and feeling they evoke. How can feeling help you live your life in more spiritual trust?

32. FLOWING INTO THE WATERS *(water)*

"In all the years when I did not know what to believe in
and therefore preferred to leave all beliefs alone,
whenever I came to a place where living water welled up,
blessedly cold and sweet and pure, from the earth's dark bosom,
I felt that after all it must be wrong not to believe in anything."

SIGRID UNDSET

TODAY I DROVE to Inverness, California, a small town an hour or so from San Francisco on Tomales Bay. Inverness is on this bay known for oyster farms and occasional shark sightings. It also is surrounded by lovely woods and beaches. To get there, I drove through Samuel P. Taylor Park and heard the bubbling water at the side of the two-lane windy road. I slowed down and finally pulled over to hear the song from the hills. I know that the drought of most summers makes this creek bed a snake of mud and that the early rains of September this year gave me this splendid melody.

When I got to Inverness, I parked my car at the side of the road where there was a line of cars. I know when I see a line of cars that an access through the woods to the bay must be near. The beach was small but clean and covered with roughly grained sand, shell pieces, and small stones, sea gulls hawing their clear cry in the breezeless air. People were wading in the cool water in the hot October sun.

I walked from one end of the beach to the other stretching my back and then remembered this beach on a day trip I took here in the early seventies. It seemed as if the years of my life had been strapped on my back, and while I gleaned from hardship and harvest, sorting and sifting my life, nothing had changed in this spot of nature. I sat and daydreamed by the shimmering, clean water. I thought how good it was that some things of beauty stayed the same even as they moved and how this dappled beach offered souvenirs of history and life braided, memories' offerings like stepping stones with the tiny pebble pieces, scattered on the blanket of beach offered to us as cashew moons.

Watching the water, I felt like I was drowning in the goddess Shiva, the Hindu goddess of love. I remembered a bit of a poem from somewhere whose sentiment said that, when drowning like this, we only want more drowning. And I thought about letting age fill my lungs with its hungry clock, my body fitting into the contours of history, earth, water, my long stride finding its pace across the sky.

I have a friend who uses the bay and ocean as her special place. Sometimes the bay fills her craving, and she disappears awhile into the spirit's shadow of rocks hanging over the wide edge of the bay. Sometimes she goes to Ocean Beach to feel its power. The ocean can hold all of her feelings. I wrote for her:

> Scream if you want to,
> the ocean takes your wailing,
> crashes grief for you until your heart is open like a tin top
> of sardines waiting for the fork of delight,
> your body alive with electricity, salt and water.

I asked her to "swagger over the badlands of happenstance triumphant." And she did.

The roar of the ocean is like the sound we hear in our mother's womb. That is why the ocean is so comforting to many people. I leave a beach feeling more balanced than when I arrived. I've always attributed that wonderful feeling to the salt air and the long-stride walk that miles of beach offer, as haven in its solitude, a reminder that we have friends beyond our tied-shoed days.

Years ago I lived on an ark at the end of a long boardwalk over a swamp. I was in a time of great upheaval, as my marriage was ending and I needed to be close to the grasses and water and to detail something life affirming. I remember having a hard time functioning, but when the creek flooded in the winter, I had to row out in my tiny boat to reach my car to get to work. In this physical exercise and the attention to detail it demanded, I found concentration on living.

I wrote the following poem during this time:

At the Edge of Land

Egrets stand on webbed feet,
lift first one and then the other
finding balance in the grasses
of this muddy flatland. The long, winding boardwalk
holds us above the mud
so we can rest
here at the creek's edge. On Saturday mornings
men repair the wooden boardwalk
from the pounding of the tide
so they can walk the night back
down the long wet planks. At the end of the day
women who don't cook
spread their meals on cracker,
hang brown trousers on the backs
of chairs near the heater's warmth. My neighbors hardly talk,
wear old straw hats low,
avoid the noon sun
and each other. The smell here takes a getting used to,
all swamp and wet.
We're on the edge of land and sea,
nowhere further to go. When the tide is in,
I sleep with water underneath me.
It soothes me, a rowing, a ping, pinging.
Water catching the four sides
in one breath, a rock, rocking. I dream of digging
eighty feet through the mud
to make a basement
find the roots of life,
make honey.

The poem is a reminder to me of how to use nature when I need replenishing. I was held by the waters of that creek which flowed into the bay and then, just a mile away, met the ocean. There I was on a creek, watching the effects of the tide; all things were connected. Without water, I knew, there is no life. Water cleanses, starts over, becomes clearer.

Water is the symbol of the life force that is ever flowing. I began to sense the truth that the waters flowed and yet held stillness for me, that spring would come and the waters would be the same and changed without my help. All I had to do was notice and write the only way I knew how. Somehow I found my way to prayer.

After Mount St. Helens erupted in 1980, the waters around it were changed forever. I heard this and was alarmed thinking of my little creek and the haven I once had on the water. In Christine Colasurdo's *Return to Spirit Lake*, she recounts not only the startling wonder of the volcanically transformed blast zone but the waters at Grizzy Lake "swelled upon receiving a heavy dose of ash and logs. . . . At the lake's west end, a waterfall tumbled in an ash-gray valley down to the lake. We were looking at what the blast zone biologists called 'lakeshore burial.' Most of the back-country lakes had experienced it—tons of ash inundating their basins to raise their bottoms and bury shoreline plants." Geological events causing both loss and new life in our living waters and land. Our job: to find a way to help out in some small way, to remember water as the symbol of life ever flowing.

Water is the home of frogs; they show us that nature is not only in accord with us but with itself. Listen at a pond and you just might hear the truth of this harmony: first one frog, then five, then fifteen, then three million croaking all at once, then quiet. Total quiet.

Water is often the symbol of the subconscious and what we have pushed aside or can't face. To go into the waters is to be reborn. I've worked with a client who in his dreams was given a fish after putting his hands in swirling water. He felt it was a symbol of beginning to know himself better.

Yesterday after attending a workshop *Going Down into the Dragon Cave*, concerning becoming whole by working with subconscious material, I dreamed I had been journaling my troubles on loose prayer pages on my lap. The wind came up and blew the prayer pages into a trough of water that was very long, as far as the eye could see and beyond. The papers, wet with ink, smeared in the water and floated at the top of the trough. I remembered thinking, "My, that's a lot of problems" and felt just fine. When I woke up I realized the water had softened them, and I felt whole. Also, because the water in the trough was so long yet shallow, little was out of my sight. Who I was seemed seen and known to me, my shadow material exposed in water and all was fine.

EXERCISES:

✦ I hope you can go to water near where you live and write a poem. It could be a pond, a fountain, a creek. Use what you have even if it's puddles after a rain. Or, fill up a bowl with water and place floating candles in it. Take a bath. Start by writing down a dozen details. The details will set the scene. Now put your feeling into it and tell a story of what you know about living your life. Read mine after you've written yours.

The Holy Grail

I wrote questions of the holy grail, the why
am I here, why am I here, as the little boat
once the ocean bobbed into the night breeze.
I asked why of everything that autumn,
wanted the world to be thrown to my feet
in answers.
When the world grew tired
of my questioning, she moved
her warmth toward the south country
leaving me with winter's breath.

Reread your poem and mine. Combine the two ideas and write a poem of the earth moving its thawing ice toward spring.

✦ If water is your old friend, your aunt, your mother-father, how are you its off-spring?

33. THE MANY POWERS OF SALT *(salt)*

"Adjectives are the sugar of literature and adverbs the salt."

THEODORA BOSANQUET

LAST NIGHT I saw the beautifully filmed movie, *Himalaya*, by director Eric Valli, which was filmed in the forbidding Dolpo region of Nepal. It's the story of a small tribe of people who earn their winter's grain by annually taking the salt they've mined across the Himalayas to the market. The yaks that carry the salt are huge and lovely animals that can bear the heavy weight of salt and are surefooted enough to traverse the dangerous, narrow trails high in the mountains. The tribespeople's lives revolve around reading the stars and trusting in signs from the gods as to whether it is a good time to embark on their dangerous yearly journey. This film reminds us that salt is a commodity that human life depends on and that people who live so close to the earth live in harmony with both this world and the next. I remember once again to pay homage to the origins of everyday things: salt, water, life. Salt, a symbol for life sustained.

Salty seawater can symbolize the bitterness in your heart. Scottish monk and mystic, Richard of St. Victor, thought we must pass through the feelings of anger and regret when we become aware of our own human state and from this state move into acceptance and joy. For the Jews, a dish of saltwater symbolized the tears shed during their long years of captivity.

Photographer John P. George talks about living within five miles of the Great Salt Lake in Utah and never thinking of the lake as anything but foul smelling and unattractive, covered with brine flies. However, once he began spending time near the lake photographing it, he began to learn about "the interweaving connections some birds have with the lake; why certain species of salt-tolerant plants were located where they were; about the nature of brine flies. What a fascinating beauty I began to notice in the mud flats, saline flats, pickleweed, shorebirds, brine shrimp, and enchanting desert islands that dominate the horizon." His photographs in *Seductive Beauty of Great Salt Lake* show the majesty of the salt encrustions on the plants protruding from the waters of the lake. Sunrise over the salt beds and the patterns of salt and gull tracks in the mud flats are lovely reminders that nature gives us everything to love. Our sense of beauty can include the saline flats at dusk and the life of beetles on jagged salt crystals. Diversity, once again ours to embrace, enriches our sight and profoundly helps the maintenance of our ecosystem.

Salt is both a preservative of food and a corrosive of metal. The phrase "the salt of the earth" was used in early times to denote aware people who could prophesy truly.

The Christians believed that the spilling of salt was directly related to the spilling of blood. By throwing a pinch of salt over your shoulder, you could put "bloodshed" behind and turn your back on any curse.

The symbol for salt sometimes comes from the fact it is a natural element of the earth, and therefore, it can stand for friendliness, wisdom, purity, and good advice or counsel.

The Romans put salt on the lips of newborns to protect them from evil spirits. (You could tell who was a pagan because they would wipe the salt off!)

The protecting and cleansing properties of salt are used in everyday life in Japan. Salt is often placed in small heaps at the entrances to houses, on the rims of wells, or scattered on the ground after funerals to protect life and safe passage. Salt may be spread at the threshold of a home once an unpleasant person leaves to cleanse the household.

Salt also symbolizes incorruptibility. At Japanese sumo wrestling matches, salt is spread as a sign of cleansing and in order that the bout be played by the rules. The Bible speaks of a "covenant of salt" as one that cannot be broken. The Children of Israel believed that eating salt and bread together sanctified a friendship that would not be broken. The ancient Greeks and Muslims, because salt is shared, thought of it as a symbol of hospitality and friendship.

I have stood at the temples of the Mayan Indians in Mexico and smelled the salt sea air humans have smelled for thousands of years. I thought of the spirit on the edge of the continent where old birds thrilled their songs and thought the air, oh, the salt air, knows where it belongs.

EXERCISES:

+ If you and your friends would do a ritual for the new year, how might you include salt? Write out a ritual and share it with your closest friends.

+ If salt can help you recognize bitterness in your heart, what would you recognize as true about yourself? Write a prayer as an antidote.

34. A LIGHT FEATHER *(feathers)*

"Fine feathers make fine birds."

LATE-SIXTEENTH-CENTURY PROVERB

THE ANCIENTS believed birds were reincarnated souls and feathers were sacred. They thought birds could fly because of the lightness of feathers. The Celts believed a feathered cloak could give the wearer lightness, speed, and the ability to travel to another world. For native North Americans, feathers were symbolic of the Great Spirit and of the sun.

We know feathers serve as insulation to birds and are replaced several times a year. Molting takes place after breeding and before migration. Sometimes during mating season, the male loses his feathers, which are replaced by colorful plumage that will attract a mate. Imagine yourself and how you "change your feathers" when you first meet a mate, or before birthing, or a long trip.

I love the way nature takes care of its own. The down feathers occasionally need to be fluffed, and this can be done by bathing in dirt. When feathers are lost, it will be just a few at a time so that balance remains. When you see birds preening themselves, they are often realigning their contour feathers so the feathers can aid in flight. Birds, flight, feathers, us, and the balance we need.

I visited a new Metropolitan Community Church forming in Berkeley, California. The sanctuary was filled with hanging, white, stenciled paper sculptures, the congregation singing a hymn about flying like an eagle, God's promise to rise again. A young man led in signing the song. (If you have been lucky enough to see someone sign for the deaf, it is uplifting. Signing is like dancing with your hands in order to communicate.) As I followed his motions, we sang the song again and again, and the song became a mantra of flight of the spirit.

I kept visualizing a feather, and in this way, a new personal symbol came to me to remind me of my source.

A client who came to me to work on abandonment issues once told me that she often carries feathers home as a remembrance of a trip outside of the city in which she lives. She says that it connects her with the place longer; the memory lasts longer. She connects in a nonverbal way with nature. I saw once again that we do these things for ourselves, not realizing that we are drawn to what helps our healing.

Author Linda Hogan would say this client is going back to the place where time unwinds, as is suggested in this passage from *Dwellings*: "Perhaps there are events and things that work as a doorway into the mythical world, the world of first people, all the way back to the creation of the universe and the small quickenings of earth, the first stirrings of human beings at the beginning of time. Our elders believed this to be so, that it is possible to wind a way back to the start of things, and in so doing find a form of sacred reason, different from ordinary reason, that is linked to forces of nature. In this kind of mind, like in the feather, is the power of the sky and thunder and sun, and many have had alliances and partnerships with it, a way of thought older than measured time, less primitive than the rational present."

Because feathers are common, it is a good symbol to bring the sacred into your everyday life. Most of our lives are spent in the ordinary, and the ordinary can be a walk on a living past, this ground of earth, the footing of our history and ancestors. It is awareness that can bring the sacred into every day. A great gift of this awareness is that you will feel in harmony with nature.

There is an Egyptian legend that says that at death the people would be weighed to see if their soul was heavy with sin. The heart of the deceased, the holder of emotions to the Egyptians, was weighed against a feather, a symbol of justice. If the two balanced, the man or woman would be blessed as they passed into the next life. On failing the test, they believed the body would soon be eaten by a creature that was part crocodile, part lion, and part hippopotamus.

To be "light as a feather" is to be without wrong doing. Even today we hear people saying "their heart felt light as a feather" after they tell the truth and lighten their load of guilt, or, when they know they have acted with integrity.

Because the feather is used in rituals as a way of blowing the sacred smoke of healing incense, the feather is itself an instrument of bringing the spirit near and is sacred in itself. Start to believe that nature and the use of symbols are not just metaphors but as alive with spirit and soul as you are. What could be true for you if you believed that nature was alive?

Exercises:

+ Because feathers help birds maintain their body heat, they are a protector of life. What blessings could you write for the natural materials that protect your life?

+ The Buddhists used prayer wheels inscribed with sacred verses called mantras. Each rotation of the cylinder stands for one recitation of the mantra. Make up a ritual for yourself using a prayer and a feather. You may be surprised how a ritual can help strengthen your beliefs and prayers.

35. WILD ROSE *(roses)*

IN THE UNITED STATES the wild rose has been used as a sign of love and respect. The Cherokee rose, state flower of Georgia, is a climbing rose with a solitary white flower. It was an early Chinese import that now grows wild throughout the south. According to legend it was given the name when a Cherokee maiden carried one of these roses to the tent of her beloved, a wounded soldier. Also, in the Civil War, the Cherokee rose was often planted as a memorial on graves of fallen soldiers by their comrades.

The wild rose was also used for eating. The following is a quotation from *Gold Rush* by J. G. Bruff: "Crossing the Sierra. September 1850—Fine morning, and we were up early. Had the fore feet of my pack-pony shod. . . . We rode along the N. side of the lake, till we reached a narrow valley, with a rapid creek. Fine tall grass, and vast quantities of rose-bushes line the margin of the stream. Their seed-pods are delight as conserve. We ate many."

As I read this journal written over 150 years ago, I recommitted myself to my personal spiritual journal, which holds my thoughts and experiences with land and sky. I realize that the journal gathers strength the more regularly I write in it, a resilience built of trusting the spirit.

The fruit of the rose is referred to as a "hip" and is usually bright red or orange. Dried hips can be used in jams, jellies, and pies. Because of its high vitamin C content, during the Second World War when oranges were scarce, European countries collected rose hips and processed them into a syrup.

I just took a walk in the parkland and saw huge bushes of wild roses bloom-ing. The roses were small and open and everywhere the color of soft red, a pink of a baby's skin, reminding me of love, and their thorns were a gentle symbol that made me remember to take care of love and help it blossom.

My friend and I walked until we were spent and then went to a photography show at the Oakland Museum. where I stood before a photograph called *Phan-tom Limb 1* by Lyn Hershman. It was a black and white image of a woman with a television screen head, very large and with the head coming forward toward me. Her description read, "We've become a society of screens, of layers that keep us from knowing the truth, as if truth were unbearable, too much for us to deal with—like our feelings—so we deal with things through replications, through copying, through screens, through facsimiles, through fiction and faction."

I felt the truth in what Hershman was saying. That could be me. In the past I didn't go out much, so caught was I in hesitation about the world. But today, no, the wonderful hillsides and the wild roses waving their tiny life to me in the breeze. I made a promise to the old person I will be someday; I will see the world firsthand to the best of my ability, noticing the everyday and what is given to me. My vow and prayer is given to live life in the clay possibilities of earth.

In Hinduism, the practitioners used a sprinkler shaped like a rose to sprin-kle rose water around the shrine of their gods, including Kali, the goddess of obstacles. This was to insure purification and to do honor to the god who gave sight and smell to mortals. Why not bathe in rose water tonight and honor yourself? You can take the petals of a rose and rub them into the water or let them float on the water. You can talk to Kali.

EXERCISES:

+ What vow can you make to the old person you will become one day?

+ In mystic symbols of alchemy and hermetic lore, the blue rose stood for impossibility, the golden rose for absolute achievement or perfection. We could consider when the blue rose has been with us and how we dealt with it. When did the golden rose raise itself to you and ask you to notice?

+ Just as the rose is a sacred female symbol, how can you find sacred the female-ness in you?

36. A BASKET OF LIFE *(baskets)*

> "A tisket, a tasket, a green and yellow basket,
> I wrote a letter to my love
> and on the way I lost it."
>
> OLD NURSERY RHYME

BASKETRY PREDATES POTTERY and was used for cooking. The Havasupai Indians in Arizona cooked seeds, mush, and meat in wicker pots lined with sandy clay. The method was to coat the curve of the loosely woven basket with clay and sand and press it into the bowl to dry. The cook then squats and shakes the food and blows on the embers to keep the food free of ash. Because baskets were used for holding nourishment, they often denoted maternal care and life.

The Navahos, although not known for their textile arts, made baskets early on. They made ceremonial baskets to hold offerings to the spirits and baskets to hold their young. They filled medicine baskets with amole root and water. They carried cacti in large baskets and made star-designed wedding baskets as gifts to the couple.

The warp and woof of basket weaving, forward and backward in the movement of the shuttle, represents time and space interacting with creation. Symbolically, thread can be thought of as the life energy stretching through time. The process of weaving can help us remember that writing stretches us to connect with the time of our ancestors and the DNA we hold and with the future of our soul's travel with us in her arms.

Because basket weaving was seen to be a feminine art, baskets are thought to be female. Like most containers, they symbolized the maternal body. A basket was seen as a holder of love that helped its owner let go of the snarls of hate.

Those of us who collect symbols for writing often have baskets holding treasures for these special times. I have a basket of rose petals and bark waiting for a ritual passage and a tiny basket of silver animal symbols from which to create stories and prayers. I made a basket to function as a bird's nest that now holds smooth pebbles from the Yuba River. Someday I'll write about flying and the wise ground of pebbles and water.

There's something spiritual about the holding of things. A basket can be associated with a mother's lap as a bowl for her child or the oasis in the desert that holds the water for life. Even the hummingbird nests outside my window in the pear tree are shaped like tiny teacup saucers, tiny enough to surround the thumb-size babies, with edges built up enough to protect them from a fall.

A friend told me about a contemporary basket she saw in the recent show at the Asian Art Museum. Sheila said, "It sent me into ether. It was a tiny thing from Japan that had a presence rarely seen in any art object, a tiny wall piece alive with energy. It was like music, like forward motion, like an anima moving to music just jumping off the wall." She said to think of it like a gesture drawing, the drawing we do in seconds just to quickly capture the motion. She was describing a basket holding the spirit of its creator, of Japanese people, and of itself: the personal and archetypal spirit.

One of the reasons to have artist friends is that they bring the life of the imagination into the everyday. This imagination, of course, is close to the spirit and close to the writer's heart and moving hand. When we read about writing about nature, we are asked again and again to really take a close look, to notice the details love gives us. We can think of a basket made of cattails and name the elements to better love it: the broad leaves, the welcoming marsh, the water of a restless lake, the seedhead freeing its seeds to the soft air, the tan color, the link between nature and the person who loves the land.

Among the lovely crafts to collect from world travels are the baskets of the peoples of different lands. The tiny Indonesian island of Sumba, is where the women make beautiful ikat, weaving with special dyes and weaving techniques known only to them. At the market just down from the Mona Lisa Hotel, you can find several generations of the same family weaving and selling their wares.

In the market on Friday night in the oldest part of Ghent, with no high buildings blocking the sky and stars, you can see forever and buy the baskets made by local women. In the night market of Chiang Mai in northern Thailand you can weave through the stalls and find silks, food, fabrics, embroidery, and baskets of brilliant colors.

Baskets can tell us a lot about the foliage and availability of natural objects of its region. In the limited, barren Aleutian Islands, some of the finest baskets—"cloth with grass" as they are called—were made into bags and as ornamentation. Colored yarns and threads were added from trade with the Russians. The coiled baskets of Eskimos in the polar regions are adorned with ivory.

The ancients thought that being contained in a basket depicts rebirth or escape from death. The basket was used for protection and to ensure everlasting life. Even today, in many religions, loved ones are buried in a container to ease their way, and there is a movement among the women's community in the United States to use straw baskets for burial in as their ancient ancestors did.

EXERCISES:

+ How can you hold different beliefs and practices from various religions and practices to weave a spiritual path of your own? Would it dilute the intent of a tradition or strengthen it for you?

+ What if the Shiva (goddess) in you is everything and holds that knowledge with respect and acts only in kindness?

+ Why not set up a basket or box that you keep as a spiritual altar for yourself. It can be a small box that travels with you, holding a small candle, an angel coin, a piece of bark, or twist of grass. As you write, you can open it and feel these symbols of the earth and heaven and know you are cared for and loved.

37. THE CALLING (bells)

> "My soul's ear catches the tiniest sound of bells,
> the movement of moss and feathers, pebbles, shells
> —this peace, an offering to memory."
>
> CAMERON SHIELDS

SHEILA WELLS, a musical friend, went to Lake Luzern in the Rigi Mountains to a tiny Swiss village, Kaltbad, at 4000 feet above sea level where the sound of bells was all around. The first morning as she woke she could hear a clanking sound, off and then on again. At breakfast she asked what the sound was and the waiter told her it was cows grazing above the village. She never saw the cows, but she could imagine the bell ringing every time a cow would lean down to graze or chew its grass. It made a lovely field of clanking all around with bells, a language to the villagers. Earlier that morning she had looked down on the first floor out of a third floor window in her hotel to see umbrella tops and the animated hum of people talking and eating on the patio shaded by the umbrellas. Bells and people, warm sun and sound filling her landscape.

She described a local concert of bell ringing given in Oakland over the holidays, recounting it through her senses, "The scene starts as a table set for a formal dinner, black table cloth and people in black tuxedoes and white gloves. Bells are stretched out in front of them like food. Each bell is brass with a golden coat and a wooden handle with its clapper inside. They make different sounds according to their size and the way the musicians pick them up and twist their wrists and hands. Putting the bell down stops the sound. Each bell makes a different sound or note; the bells are like voices. The musicians move their two hands and interweave according to the music written down in front of them, which looks like drumming music because so many of the same notes are repeated in rhythmical patterns." Sounds before voices, our ancient heritage.

Bells have long been associated with mystical happenings and communication with spirits. Goddess images in the shape of a bell have been saved from very ancient times. It is believed they were used in ritual and worship. Magical powers were assigned to bells because they were positioned between earth and heaven, reminding us of the passage between the two worlds. Christian bells, made of silver, were used to summon worshippers to mass.

Bells were also used for protection. The church bells were rung during thunderstorms to scare away demons that were threatening to enter into peoples' lives by using thunder and lightning. We find bells used in exorcisms and in rites of excommunication, such as in Shakespeare's reference to "bell, book, and candle" in *King John, III*. Ancient Hebrew priests wore robes fringed with gold bells to protect them as they entered and left the temples. Native South American shamans used bells to protect themselves from evil influence as they worked their magic.

In the United States we have our Liberty Bell in Philadelphia which signifies freedom and the liberty for which our foremothers and forefathers fought. We use school bells to call children to order and to learn, which is a part of our right, the right to a free and democratic education not overlain with religion.

In African-American belief, bells have been used in healing as objects capable of driving away stuttering. They once believed drinking from a bell and giving oneself to its clear, pure tone could cure stuttering. The bell was widely regarded as passing good news such as at weddings or victories. Small tinkling bells can be used for the sound of happiness and pleasure, yet the bell can mark the passage of time as in the death toll.

Bells can be seen to embody movement. Here's a short poem I wrote reminding us that time is on our side as we delve deeper into our spiritual journey through writing.

Movement

Let your body move itself
to Wednesday, Thursday. Friday
lift your head to the tinkle of the bell

in a snowflake. Saturday, wrap yourself
in the spread of your bed.
Sleep Sunday in warm silence.
Let time take you to the next door.

Bells can symbolize a calling or a time for change. I once belonged to a neighborhood spirit circle at which a large bell making a deep sound was rung at the beginning and end of the ritual. Tiny, tinkling bells sounded as a signal to the passageways between parts of the ritual. For example, stones were washed by each woman signifying release and renewal, and then a tiny bell was rung to indicate the finish and a return to our seats. New commitments were written. The tiny bell sounded time to share commitments and put the writings into a communal nesting bowl. The deep bell told us of the ritual's end, indicating time to share a meal.

The use of bells made me feel that I was part of something ancient. It helped me realize that my intent was important and the sharing in a community way made my wishes seem more possible. The ritual was a reminder to be faithful to soul and talent.

Just to hear a bell can signify protection or the heralding of care. It can mean whatever you want it to mean today and can be a simple pleasurable ritual in your life as you sit down to write—a ring of a bell and you are reminded you are never alone in the heart.

EXERCISES:

✦ Imagine you have a commitment bowl that you place on your table; what would some of those commitments be? How would you use bells?

✦ As we answer the call of our spirit, we must come to terms with feminism and spirituality. We must first develop an adult self and take that to spirituality. How can we learn to speak up yet do contemplative prayer? How can we learn our own desires yet detach from our ego's wanting? How can we develop a self yet understand the concept of self negating? How could the sound of a bell keep us in this delicate balance?

✦ The call of the bell can go everywhere there is spirit, and spirit is everywhere. Perhaps you've seen Hindu or Buddhist statues with gods of many arms. These symbolize all they can do for devotees. What are the many ways that the spirit can hold you?

38. WHITE BREATH *(winter)*

> "In a way winter is the real spring,
> the time when the inner thing happens,
> the resurge of nature."
> EDNA O'BRIEN

IN THE GREEK MYTH of Persephone, winter is a time when the world is in mourning. The trees and the ground are bare, waiting for the young woman who was kidnapped and taken to the underworld against her will for eating the food of the seven pomegranate seeds, a food that is thought not fit to eat. She must be kept in dark confinement and cannot be returned totally to the earth. As partial forgiveness, when spring comes she is allowed to be with her family, and the warmth and color of her life return to her. However, winter is always waiting.

And so we must decide: will we face winter as a cold that will pierce our heart or will it be a gift for the hibernating soul that finds peace in solitude? How much will we struggle against it? What symbol will we give it? Does winter hold our life, and is it active, or are we waiting for the green growth of the bulb to show us birth and growing again? Is it all right to have a "waiting time"? Or, as in the myth of Persephone, is winter a punishment?

I treasure Patricia Hampl's view of winter: "The cold was our pride, the snow was our beauty. It fell and fell, lacing day and night together in a milky haze, making everything quieter as it fell, so that winter seemed to partake of religion in a way no other season did, hushed, solemn." Or anthropologist Margaret Mead's: "Blackberry winter, the time when the hoarfrost lies on the blackberry blossoms; without this frost the berries will not set. It is the forerunning of a rich harvest." I also understand Jane Gillespie talking from a mother's point of view, remembering winter days that felt endless with a young restless child: "In our part of the world winter is the normal state of affairs and seems to last five years. This is fine for the skiers, but by the end of March all gardeners and mothers have begun to go mad."

In David Fontana's *The Secret Language of Symbols* he writes, "Ice symbolizes sterility, coldness and rigidity, in humans and in nature. The melting of ice therefore heralds the return of life. Snow shares something of this symbolic meaning; however, being soft and beautiful, it also stands for latent truth and hidden wisdom."

A friend remembers climbing over 14,000 feet to the summit of Mt. Shasta in the snow, using an ice axe and crampons. He started out at 4 A.M., when the moon was full, to start the trip that would end fourteen hours later. He said it sharpened his perception to cover the terrain when risk was a factor. He knew snow in a convex shape might break off and cause an avalanche. Steep, loose snow could also be unstable. He noted what the Russians call "sastrugi," or the wind ridge that sculpts and packs the snow, and enjoyed the changing shapes of nature. That night he had the deepest sleep of his life, the kind of sleep that comes from being outside with beauty, physical exertion, and accomplishment.

I thought of how the snow takes the place of apple blossoms. How in our world we make meaning by how we interpret reality. The time of cold can be positive or negative depending on how we view it. One year, teaching in Illinois, I had to shovel my car out to get to school and drive on the slippery roads, occasionally sliding into other cars. Yet, I also remembered the school "snow days" and curling up in bed with a good book, allowing snow to be a messenger from the winter skies of a need to rest. I remember shoveling out our car on New Year's Day to get to the hospital where my sister was giving birth to my only nephew. On the other side of shoveling and cold I was given a baby to love.

As I returned last holiday season to my sister's home in Youngstown, Ohio, I found the beauty of snow tucked into the turn of the branches and on the high sides of the tree nodules in Mill Creek Park. I put on my once-a-year snow boots and tramped through the woods surrounded by maple, buckeye, and cedar. The evergreens seemed to have been sprayed with white, like in a Christmas tree lot. The snow was several feet high, and a small path had been shoveled out by the park rangers. For that day, it was untouched and a wonderland for a wanderer who dared to face up to the cold and dream poetry.

I remembered when my sister and I were about ten and eleven years old, we went out back on one of the coldest days of the year and built an igloo out of the snow that had been falling and gathering for the past two weeks. Snow now lay firmly packed with gray soot in its white. As we worked, snow flurries were thickening the ground by inches. Our gloves were wet and our fingers practically frozen as we finished the little ice hut. Only one of us could fit in it at a time, and we almost froze taking turns. The roof was quite low and unstable, and it was just as cold inside as outside in those few testing moments we gave it. It was one of the first times I realized the making of something was important and not the actual result. It was the training ground for making art and creativity and for spirituality seen as a process.

But that day in Youngstown, as I walked through the woods, I thought of where the soul might live in this city park. I remember once reading in a poem by Anne Sexton that in the snow each branch wears a sock for God. This passage reminded me that we can think of snow as a gift from the heavens to quiet our world: to stay inside and read and reflect. To appreciate a time of slowing down may be the salvation of snow.

A week later I returned to Chicago after an absence of twenty-five years, and I was surprised how everything in my near north neighborhood was both different and the same. There had been thirty-two inches of snow that December, and the brownstone houses up and down Roscoe Avenue looked like a picture postcard. I arrived late at night and, after talking to my friends, went straight to bed. I awoke in the morning to a familiar but forgotten sound: the scraping against the pavement as snow was shoveled. The scrape, the silence as the snow is thrown, the scrape. It was a sound that reminded me of all the joys of living in a section of the country with true seasons. I seemed to come alive through the sound. I felt childlike and filled with luckiness.

Even the sound of stamping off my feet as I went inside the back door was a sound that I had forgotten and that sent me reminders of a spiritual connection to the earth. How fortunate I am to have had the land and the weather of Ohio and Illinois in me! How thankful I am to have lived long enough to work through difficult times to now give praise to what I was given.

Lake Michigan is a winter playground. Although I don't remember if there are trout there, my imagination wrote this stanza for a poem as I watched ice fishing and ice skating from the edge of the frozen lake:

In the winters of a lake, everything has its place,
a fisherman pulls up his hard-bodied trout
knowing to lay the meat,
tough from struggle,
on ice a few days. The lake is shoveled clean
for lovers
who show up brave at twilight
to skate their zigzagged lines fast as a breath.

Winter is also used commonly as the "season" of maturity and wisdom, or decline and old age. We can decide what we want to use as symbols for the "winter" of our life. We can be aware when age comes on tiptoes and leaves its marks on us. We can hum the tunes of our times and enjoy them. I thought of my deceased father as I dreamed in the snowy winter of the midwest and wrote this poem for the man who loved his quiet walks in nature in any season of the year.

Hereafter

You could be swinging on a hammock
nibbling a pear, your feet naked
to the balmy coast, aware that you were directed
to this. You could have nothing to fear. Your death

and its pain over. Worry ceased. Loved one left
to care for each other. Look at what you're offered—
the ripe summer opening its nectar and its rose
to you, the valley winds

blowing its reminder of nesting, that expanse of white
things: birds, the bear, cousin of egrets.
Why shouldn't you be the breeze over Barcelona
enjoying the clay land and quiet
outskirts, the solitude you longed for without the loneliness.

In the East, the inner journey has often been taken more seriously, and the positive bias for the culture has been for the introvert; winter there is a symbol of a rich time. From this part of the world comes symbolism of incubation periods: a time devoted to cutting off conscious thought to make connection with the inner self. This can be seen as the time of "sleeping in temples," as many religious followers actually do.

EXERCISES:

✦ How has sound been important to you in your spiritual journey? What sound reminds you that you are spirit housing a body?

✦ How can you visualize the "winter" of your life? What do you hope to be your thoughts and feelings?

39. TURTLE, TORTOISE, AND TERRAPIN *(the three)*

> "Rise up, my love, my fair one, and come away.
> For, lo, the winter is past, the rain is over and gone;
> The flower appears on the earth; the time of the singing bird is come,
> and the voice of the turtle is heard in our land."
>
> SONG OF SOL. 2:10

THE NATURALIST Jack Rudloe, in his book *Search for the Great Turtle Mother*, is intrigued by a legend recounted by fishermen in Costa Rica. A turtle-shaped rock, normally pointed out to sea, turned to face inland when it was time for the turtles to come ashore to nest. "The Turtle Mother rock functioned as the intermediary between humanity and nature, as a control mechanism to prevent overfishing," writes Rudloe. He seeks to prove this myth and ends up sleeping among the turtles with his exploration team. He writes, "We talked into the night, lying beside the turtles in the shack on stilts. . . . It was quite a cacophony of snores and turtle gasps. It was hard to tell who snored worse, the turtles or members of our expedition. We were sharing the space with two greens and two hawksbill, each of which made occasional loud gasps and hisses like someone blowing through a straw." He has other wonderful turtle stories in this book, but I won't spoil the ending for you by telling you if he proves the myth of our ancestors or not.

Turtles, tortoises, and terrapins are an ancient and closely related family of reptiles, having lived on this planet since the age of dinosaurs. They have changed little over 200 million years and can be found throughout the world.

Cold-blooded, they regulate their body temperature internally although bask-
ing in the sun can raise their body temperature too. Tortoises usually live on
land, terapins in fresh water (or as pets in a freshwater fish tank) and all turtles
but one live in the sea.

The "giant" tortoises of the Galapagos Islands can reach five feet in length and
can weigh 200–300 pounds. They were first discovered by pirates, who used
them as a food source on their adventures. Later, whale ships and sealing ships
would take thousands of tortoises on board for their meat on long journeys.
Because of the introduction of dogs that ate the tortoises' eggs and goats that
ate the tortoises' food on the islands, the tortoise is now in danger of becoming
extinct. We need to save all sentient creatures but particularly one so much in
mythology and history, symbolizing the world itself and holding female creation and fertility within its form.

Tortoises are regarded as benevolent creatures and are thought to have enormous wisdom because of their wrinkled skin and features. The body of a turtle
or tortoise holds many symbolic meanings. Its shell represents the world, the
curved upper part the dome of the skies and heaven, the flat lower part the
earth. Its legs, sturdy and stumpy, symbolize determination and great age. The
turtle shell was often used in ancient rituals depicting heaven and earth joining
together.

The ancient name for North America is Turtle Island, the continent that was
carried on the back of a turtle. Native Americans often believed that the people who kept their history alive through storytelling and symbols were "the turtle people" because they carried tradition on their backs. In Indian sign
language, in order to say turtle first you would make the sign *walk*, then *with*,
then *house;* then you would show the size. Stone sculptures of turtles were
believed to preserve the stability of the world.

In the fable "The Hare and the Tortoise," the tortoise became famous for its
slow but steady movements. In this tale steadiness and consistency were the
traits that helped the tortoise win the race over the fast-moving hare. The tale
reminds us that slow but steady wins the race and that various traits can be to
our advantage if we use them well.

In psychology, a turtle symbolizes quiet strength and protection if there
should be an attack, because it can withdraw into itself. In Native American cultures, the turtle is thought to demonstrate the superiority of quick wit over

brute force. In a typical tale, the turtle defeats his stronger opponent in a tug-of-war by taking his end of the rope and tying it around an even stronger animal. Have you used the qualities attributed to the turtle to gain in your spiritual life?

In the North American cultures the turtle was widely used for folk medicine because of its symbolic value of persistence and perseverance. In their turtle dances, the turtle is a symbol of the feminine and fertility and dancers wear turtle shells and rattles. In Mexico the use of turtle shells as drums was common. The turtle carapaces were struck with antler, stick, or another hard implement and could call for thunder when rain was needed.

EXERCISES:

+ If you did a dance of female blessing, what would you honor in yourself?

+ Do you withdraw when you feel afraid? What are your options to this behavior? When does withdrawal help your spiritual life?

+ Find a small sculpture or a picture of a tortoise or draw a tortoise totem. How can you use this image as a personal symbol?

40. BLOOMS *(flowers)*

"Arranging a bowl of flowers in the morning
can give a sense of quiet in a crowded day—
like writing a poem, or saying a prayer."

ANNE MORROW LINDBERGH

A TALENTED VIOLINIST, Sara, told me the story of seeing a blooming magnolia tree that helped her perform on her violin without feeling a familiar fear of performance anxiety. She was playing chamber music, and because of her fear of exposure she found it hard to hold on to her love of music. She looked out the window and up into the tree, and she told me that it was as if blooms were brought to her sight; there was an intense green offering with huge pink flowers. It was a vision that brought the memory of how she is connected. She felt safe. It was like that green and those blooms helped her say, "Oh yeah, I'm here. I'm part of this. Music is a part of this." She stepped beyond her petty concerns of exposure and returned more to the truth. Her eyes welled up with tears and she continued, "I so often waver between remembering that and feeling lost. I forget why I am here and then the light in the tree or a gorgeous pink blossom comes to sight and I relax. It's beyond words. I've been shown something."

I asked Sara if sound in nature held the world together for her. She said it did, because what you're hearing is where you are. "The birds say you are here. Right here. The rustling of the leaves in the princess trees showing off their purple flowers. There, you are right where you are. What you hear is more information about yourself and the world. The sound of music too. Sound places you. I actually like the deeper, richer tones of the violin; my ear looks for a smooth kind of richness, a dark and sort of mellow quality. I find the rich warmth of the violin and drop into that awareness. With the bow over the strings I can feel what's needed to produce sounds. It's a physical feeling," she told me. Like gardening, I thought. Like weeding in an English garden through the hollyhock and petunias, coaxing the roses to life. Hearing the breeze and the bell tower in the background.

Novelist Madeline Moore told me of growing up in Lousiana where flowers flourished in abundance: azaleas with their enormous purple bloom and red camellias in the manicured yard of the neighbor woman who gave her candy. The smell of white gardenias coming from across the street from Mrs. East's garden and given to Madeline as wrist corsages as she grew older and went to dances.

There is something about flowers that begs gift and giving. When I was just a little child living on Barwell Street in Akron, Ohio, I borrowed my mother's sewing scissors and cut lilac blossoms from the neighbor's bush three doors down. I remember most of the branches being too thick to cut, so I tore them off and wondered just once if that were okay. I then went around selling them for two cents a bunch to neighbors, including the people from whose tree I took them. A hurried phone call and my dad came and explained commerce and fairness.

The flower is generally a symbol of nature's gift, speaking to life's transitions and its delights. This idea is expressed in the ancient practice of scattering flower petals over the dead. Marigolds were ancient offerings to the dead on November 1, The Day of the Dead, All Souls' Day. A flower that blooms a second time is a symbol for safe return and often used on altars in Christian services to show the risen Christ. The second bloom of flowers may deepen your belief that nothing is lost, everything is used again and again.

The flower's structure may look like a mandala, which symbolizes full creation. This likeness links the flower to the powers of the sun, the soul, the self, and the spirit. Sometimes flowers are seen as spring, youth, dawn, feminine virtue, and purity. Because they hold dew and rain, they are seen as being given the gifts of heaven.

Different parts of the flower have varying symbolic meanings. The blossom is often associated with grace, the rod is divine approval, the flower is the vitality of life, the branch is continued vitality.

Flowers often forecast the coming of spring or summer. I remember the Hurley's yard around the corner because every March or April the crocuses would come up through the end of the snow. I thought it a miracle. From David Carrol's diary, *Trout Reflections*: "Pussy willows full in bloom in the hollows. Their silver-white flowers hold yellow pollen, and they shed black buds scales down on her as I brush through them. These heavily cat-skinned shrubs show a trust in the season's advance."

One particularly long and cold winter in the Midwest, my son was wanting warm weather so he could play outside. We planted artificial flowers in the snow bank outside the kitchen window to remind spring to hurry and come. We decided the earth might see and feel these flowers and hear his prayer. When the world opened her arms to warmth and flowers, he felt he helped in spring's coming.

For years it was thought that the reason for the bright color of flowers was to attract insects that, in turn, are useful for pollinating. It turns out, however, that the lovely smell of the blooms is what attracts the insects. Some flowers emit ultraviolet rays that insects can see better than color.

The sunflower was so named from a Greek myth that says, according to Phyllis Busch's *Wildflowers*, that "there was a water nymph named Clytie who decided one day to leave the ocean and visit land. Clytie climbed to the top of Mount Olympus. There she saw the sun god Apollo and fell madly in love with him. But he loved someone else, and this made her very sad. Day after day, she did nothing but gaze at the sun from dawn to dusk—until she sank into the earth, developed roots, and changed into a flower. As the plant grew and blossomed, it always turned its face toward the sun, reflecting the rays of Clytie's beloved, Applo. Because of this the plant was named Sunflower (Helianthus annus). The genus name comes from two Greek words, *helios* (sun) and *anthos* (flower)."

Here are some examples of a flower code that lovers used from a guide G. W. Gessmann wrote in 1899 as listed in the *Dictionary of Symbolism*:

Red Carnation: You will be able to resist no longer, once you see the extent of my esteem.

Clover (Four-leaf): Fortune smiles open me when I can share it with you.

Dahlia: My heart is eternally with you, the heart is a homeland, not of body.

Hyacinth (white): My heart draws me to you, pale dreamer.

Lavender: The memory of you is my only quiet joy.

Lilac: In your every look and word speaks the beauty of your soul.

Nasturtium: How shall I suffer, when the prospect of seeing you
no longer fills my spirit with joyful hope!

Rose-petal (red): This is the pledge of love and fidelity.

Rose-petal (white): Its pale petals signify to you the joy of love eternal
and pure, for it lacks all earthly glow.

Rosebud (with thorns): Love, hopeful, with the doubts of uncertainty.

Of course, given the varying meanings a same flower could carry, the lovers
must agree on their meanings of the code.

There is plenty of pre-Raphaelite flower imagery in Shakespeare's *Ophelia*.
Here is the story, as found in Miranda Bruce-Mitford's *The Illustrated Book of
Signs and Symbols*: "Driven to madden by her beloved Hamlet's murder of her
father, Ophelia drowns herself in a stream. The garlands in her hair and the
flowers that surround her are all charged with symbolic meaning. The willow
represents forsaken love; the nettle growing in its branches represents pain; and
the daisies near Ophelia's hand are symbolic of innocence. The chain of violets
around her neck is associated with faithfulness, chastity, and untimely death.
The poppy is also a symbol of death; other flowers floating in the water are
linked to sorrow; and the forget-me-nots on the bank are an entreaty not to forget Ophelia."

In art school, students are asked to look beyond the names or labels of things
to see the shape, color, or form of the object so that they might draw it uniquely.
This is a good way to open your mind and not allow the naming to be limiting. However, we are naming things in nature to bring them closer to us. We
allow lilies of the valley and their scent to live in our heart. We draw our first
breath with the morning glories and close our eyes to star jasmine. A single
daffodil can remind us that spring is on its way and with the skirts of spring,
change and warmth, fields of mustard. To name things makes them more real;
the mustard grass of California's wine country, the Queen Anne's lace of New

Jersey, the orchids of Hawaii are companions reminding us we are connected to the earth.

Exercises:

+ Ask your loved ones and friends what their favorite flowers are and see what they symbolize to them. What about yourself?

+ Give someone you love an unexpected bouquet and save a bloom for yourself. What does it symbolize to you?

+ If the spirit used flowers to remind us of beauty in the world, how can beauty remind us of spirit?

41. SWEET TREATS *(fruit)*

"He that would eat the fruit must climb the tree."
EARLY-EIGHTEENTH-CENTURY PROVERB

MUCH OF THE SYMBOLISM for fruit comes from its traditionally feminine aspects: smoothness, roundness, ripeness. As a gift from the fertility goddess, the symbol of ripeness and abundance, fruit contains the seeds of the beginning of life. Fruit can be seen as the beginning of creation and potential. Because of its round shape and full "belly," the fruit of the pear tree is often considered mother love and feminine love. In ancient times, as today, fruit was valued for its nourishing moisture and as a source of sweetness.

Once I went with neighbors to take our children to pick apricots in the orchards of the Sacramento valley. It was a scorching summer day and the apricot trees were laden with fruit. The color of the pale orange fruit against the green foliage was startlingly beautiful. The smell of sweet fruit filled the air. My young son ate until he felt sick and then lay down in the car to sleep. I left the orchards feeling very close to the offerings from the land, even though my son didn't remember much of the day and couldn't stand to eat another apricot for years.

The fruit is the culmination of the tree's process. Symbolically, in Christianity, to taste the fruit of the Tree of Knowledge is to learn the difference between good and evil. To taste the fruit of the Tree of Life is to learn of your own mortality. It is your lesson in the finite nature of life.

"Fruits with seeds such as pomegranate, orange, lemon, melon, or gourd carry archetypal meanings of fertility and self potential," writes Miranda Bruce-Mitchell in *The Illustrated Book of Signs and Symbols*. "In Japan," she continues, "the cherry is associated with self-sacrifice, particularly in relation to samurai warriors—the red fruit of the cherry symbolizing blood. . . . The pineapple is a life-giving fruit and a symbol of fertility. In many parts of America pineapples were a sign of hospitality and sailors would place a pineapple on the gatepost to tell neighbors that they were home from sea. . . . In the Far East the plum is a symbol of ripening female sexuality . . . grapes are a symbol of revelry, and the orange good fortune and fertility."

A client tells me that in Judaism the lemon represents feeling or the human heart. In the Celtic spiritual rites, the lemon had power that could protect and provide an antidote to harmful thoughts and deeds. The peach also had protective powers against wrong doing and was a symbol of life everlasting.

Fruit trees can make tree climbing more fun! A friend remembers competing with the birds one summer in a wild cherry tree and the feelings of delight to be so close to nature. He had his first feelings of independence up in this tree.

The thrill to find a wild fruit safe to eat has been felt by many of us who have been lucky enough to wander through a deciduous forest. The wild persimmons! The persimmons fall first, probably to help birds and raccoons to find the ripe fruit and thereby spread the seeds around. I want to believe the leaves also fall first to protect the ripe and falling fruit.

EXERCISES:

✦ When have you been connected to orchards or growing things? How has this been good for your spiritual life?

✦ What are some of the "fruits" of your life so far?

✦ There is a tradition of a folding book in Burmese Buddhism that accordion-folds into a word and picture story called a *parabaik*. A *parabaik* tells the story of the Buddha on his way to the bodhi tree where he attained enlightenment or a story like this. Perhaps you could tell a twofold story of the fruits of your enlightment by making yourself a *parabaik*.

42. LITTLE ONE *(acorns)*

> "Somewhere a child is planting an acorn
> and dreams of living in a grand oak tree."
>
> SHERRILL CRAWFORD

I REMEMBER writing a poem once that said in part, "The spirit loves the crawling child in Jesus." Even if we don't believe in Jesus, we can know that in Christianity and in many religions, the symbol for humanity was the small one, the one who needed time to learn and grow. The acorn touches our archetypal imagination and makes the acorn a symbol of great growth and maturing.

I always found it a comfort to realize that as we are born a small one, we do not have to be perfect. Rather, we are supposed to use our years to understand ourselves and the world. The poem I wrote, by the way, ended in a passage that says instead of church, "I'll take my Sundays with the swamp grass and the mud." I would love it if acorns from an oak were there too.

In Christian religions, the acorn was seen as a symbol of truth. One way of testing love was to place two acorns in water; if they floated apart, there could be trouble coming.

Alison Jones writes in the *Dictionary of World Folklore:* "Because of their unusually long period of maturation (up to three years) and the fact that they only appear on mature (oak) trees, acorns have traditionally represented the fruition of labor and patience and have symbolized, in convenient folkloric shorthand, a long period of time. An example is the common proverb 'Great oaks from little acorns grow,' urging the listener to take the long view, that seeming insignificant labors will bear much fruit in the future. One German folktale tells how a peasant outwits the devil in a Faustian soul bargain by promising to deliver himself when his first crop should be harvested, and by plant-ing acorns wins himself a considerable respite."

My mother used to say that sometimes you hand an acorn over a fence and they hand you back a pine cone. In those days, her world was of the house and backyard, young children and neighbors. She used this expression when neigh-bors heard something she said in a way that was not what she meant. It was an early lesson that we can't help how others take what we say. It's part of not knowing how things will turn out. We expect one thing and get another.

I recently saw a print of photographer Ruth Bernhard's of a doll's head in a wooden hand. She talked about seeing a doll's head in a second-hand store and buying it without knowing how she would use it. Several days later she saw a large, wooden hand holding Turkish cigarettes and asked the man behind the cigar counter if she could buy it or use it as a prop. The inscription on the photo, called *Doll's Head,* read, "When you get that kind of message you're not allowed to say no." I think of my mom talking in such visual, concrete terms and feel there is a photograph in her symbols of acorn exchanged for a pine cone. Symbols, images in the backyards of our life.

In *Folklore, Mythology and Legend,* Maria Leach writes about the acorn dance or feast: "The autumn feast of the Hupa Indians of California, the coast Yuki, and other northwest, California tribes: a first-feast ceremony of these people. A special group of women is appointed to gather, grind, and leach the acorns and make them into a mush. At noon on the day of the feast the people gather to await the coming of the priest. But they must not look at him as he approaches the feast-ground because he impersonates Yinukatsisdai, the god of vegetation. He builds the ceremonial fire and heats the stones with which to cook the mush. When everyone has eaten, he then burns all the leftovers with prayers that the new crop not be eaten by rodents. The stones are never used again, and never touched by anyone but the priest, who piles them up in order year after year."

EXERCISES:

✦ Consider asking several friends over to cook a vegetarian mush and to say prayers to the earth and spirit for their rewards. What kind of ritual might you do?

✦ When have you felt like the tiny acorn protected by the giant oak? When have you done that for another? How does your spirit give you permission to learn and grow?

✦ I have a friend who was raised a Catholic and married a man from India and practiced the Hindu religion for the twenty years she was married to him. After his death, she moved back to the states and started going to a neighborhood Buddhist temple. Recently she asked her teacher if it was all right that she found herself praying to Jesus Christ during meditation, and the teacher said, "A good man. Continue." How does the religion of your childhood enter into your spirited practice of today?

43. BLAZING FIELDS *(fields)*

> "First flowers bloom all around me; the ground is now
> fertile and turned. Winter's dross has been baled on
> the hillside and to purify soon will be burned. Spring fever
> has reached a high frenzy, emotions soon will let go;
> that all things in nature be fertilized, in field after field will they sow.
> For the Harvest of fall is now planted; what we will need now
> must be done—in this time of greatest fertility—
> when in nature two are now one. And the wheel turns on."
>
> WICCA SPELL FOR BELTANE,
> THE TRADITIONAL FERTILITY FESTIVAL

WHAT WE PUT into our mouths is our most direct, daily link to the earth and its fields. The spirit does not live apart from the earth but is in our earth feeding us. In Judaism, the Matzoh, the flat unleavened bread, is eaten as a reminder of the food provided and the haste in which the Israelites fled from Egypt. Bread symbolizes spiritual nourishment. It is the food of the body and soul. Christians talk about the "bread of life" that worshippers partake of at communion. The ceremonial "breaking of bread" may once have symbolized the death of the sacrificed victim or, in modern times, a meeting of the minds or friendship.

In *Diet for a Small Planet,* Frances Moore Lappe tells us that there is no reason for famine; grain is abundant, and in grain alone there is enough food for all of us. We can all be provided with grain from the heartbeat beneath our feet: hunger is less about nature's limits than human habits. Lappe feels our goal must be to enable all countries to grow their own grain for human consumption.

We have the power of the pen in our vote. This would be spirituality in action.

Sometimes I think it is our language and the way we talk that makes us separate from the spiritual giving and wonder of the earth. We do not know *wheat*. We do not know how to talk to it and have it talk to us. When I think of the definition of *God* as being to invoke or call, I yearn to know the mystery of how to call back a language of creation.

The symbol of grain is the food that the earth gives us: abundant and plenty. It is a symbol for life's nourishment. It is the corn blowing in the fields of Iowa that asks us to lie down in her wealth and feast. Try writing from your body that knows fullness and hunger, emptiness and spirit, and write a prayer to the earth that all stomachs could be filled. This is what I call writing from the vital, the body that knows.

I do like reading that the earth is unlimited. Although the earth is fragile, I want to have time to change and help in greening our land and earth. Albert Schweitzer believed that any religion that doesn't respect life is not really spiritual and that until we learn to love and have compassion for the earth and all living things, we will not find contentment. He said that the earth is abundant and the fertile fields that live on it serve us in a partnership. By writing this book, I try to do my part just as you do by reading of how to dwell on this earth with heart and caring. As we write out these exercises, we give homage to the earth.

My friend Mari remembers playing at her grandparent's farm in the middle of the state of Minnesota in summer and the warm, musty smell of corn fields. They were higher than her head and she could play for hours hidden in their sweet smell. She remembers when she'd pick an ear how scratchy the stalk was and how the ear of corn was protected by silk that was moist.

There was a grain bin, which was a room six by eight feet that was sealed very tightly so the mice couldn't get in. She'd often be able to squeeze into the room and put her hand in the oats and touch the cool, fine, and slippery oats. She could smell the sweet, musty smell and sometimes would sit on it; other times she helped her grandfather shovel it and felt comforted and safe being so close to the land and her grandfather. And plenty to eat!

She remembered her grandfather talking about trying to plant as far down below the breeze as they could to ensure a warmer place for the flax. She could look out the window of her bedroom at morning's light and find an intense field of cobalt blue as far as her eye could see. The wind would wave patterns in the late afternoon, and the flax would have soft, rounded edges and a soft whishing sound. When she wears linen today, she remembers those hot summer days loving the fields of blue.

A friend, Madeline, who is an introvert raised in a family of extroverts, often felt overwhelmed by the activity and nonsense of her family. At five she found a place where she felt safe and content in a vacant field next door. There was an area of rich, soft, slightly wet dirt, and every day she would get a stick and make a circle. She would then sit inside her circle and say, "This is my land," and, "Over there, that is my mother and father's house." It made her very happy to be in her own land and also not to be them. Today she is a novelist and a person of great imagination.

Most American fields and grasslands are west of the Great Lakes because they can survive without the rainfall that tree land needs. The region is planted with grains and makes wonderful birdwatcher vistas with the fields' uninterrupted view. Perching birds can use their strong, flexible toes, three pointing forward and one backward, to grasp even a blade of grass. Tiny nests may be found on the floor of the earth, holding their spring yield. Wide, open, and vast, the fields symbolize to many of us open space and abundance.

Fields of grain are universally used as symbols of the earth's unbounded gift to us of plenty. Grain is a very fortunate symbol in dream imagery because it denotes happiness and abundance. To see freshly harrowed and plowed fields in a dream may symbolize that you will soon reap the benefits of your hard work.

Buddhist thought reminds us that sentient beings have a life connected and yet separate from our will and our doing. They would say a field of crops grows itself to spring. Farmers farm, ready for harvesting: plant, fertilize, weed, and water the fields. But when the tied string of the winter is over, the spring field feeds its own tender roots under the spirit's skies, like a baby taking milk from the mother allowing itself safe sleeping, time to grow.

EXERCISES:

+ Seeing can be an automatic process. If we see an old tractor, scarecrow, or tree in the fields, because we are caught by the opposite contrasts of old and new, we may wake up and see the fields anew. When have you noticed the old against the young, the rough against the smooth, the light against the dark? Start a page in your journal when contrast helps you see better.

✦ If fertile fields are the symbol for an abundant life, what grows in your field?

✦ Write something vital as an act of courage.

44. THE WINDY RIVER *(rivers)*

> "A river seems a magic thing. A magic, moving, living part
> of the very earth itself—for it is from the soil, both from the depth
> and from its surface, that a river has its beginning."
>
> LAURA GILPIN

RIVERS SHARE in the general symbolism of water and fluid life. For the river's roles in nourishing and providing transportation and protection (a boundary) for humans, rivers have been regarded as sacred and worshipped as spirits who also fertilize the earth they pass.

With a sense of pride, we can see that rivers are remarkable reminders of how America once was, and still is, in fewer and fewer places. Rivers are fragrant reminders of the milk of our heritage. They also remind us that in the flowing river there is the hidden stillness of life. Rivers can be stretched out reserves overflowing with promise, home to trout, steelhead, and perch. The birds live at the river: eagle, kingfisher, heron; also the otter, alligator, and beaver.

In a movie directed by Robert Redford, *A River Runs Through It*, the scenes of the sparkling water could change a city lover into a river seeker. The sun shined brilliantly on the rapidly flowing water as if a piece of the world opened and invited us to become vital again. The river was like the best of our energy when we love and sparkle of all that there is.

Wild and energetic rivers remind me of my aliveness. I also loved the quiet, meandering river of my childhood, the Cuyahoga River, running between Cuyahoga Falls and Akron, Ohio, flowing on to Cleveland. It was clean, gently flowing water then. (Later, parts of the Cuyahoga River became so full of oil from industry that the water caught on fire!) Grand, flat granite rocks spread themselves on either side, seeming to me a container for the water. I would lie on my tummy and write in my journal. The overgrowth of trees at the banks provided me with a sense of privacy as I wrote my young feelings and was part of the scene's charm.

I believe the river's charm and stillness allowed me to go into a peaceful trance or meditation; I wrote sideways and at right and left angles, ideas connecting feelings to thought, feelings to feelings with slanted phrases and circular ideas. I'd go home and "straighten" it up and make sense of it, but I remember that nonlinear writing as making total sense to me.

Don't you think writing of our youth helped form who we are today? People who are reflective, aware of our surroundings and how the world comforts us. I walk down twenty-fourth Street in San Francisco where I have my counseling practice and there is no lovely river in sight. But there are puddles after a rain, flower boxes on window sills, bottle brush with its lovely red bloom living well in redwood containers placed on the sidewalks, and the feeling of rain in the air at the end of some days. I could lie at that river bank once again and be content. I hope you had a river or a special place to write and explore who you were. If not, let's find you one!

There was another river from my childhood that was important to me. Summers, we went to visit my grandmother in Moline, Illinois, and watch the Mississippi River travel through that part of the tri-cities country. I was mesmerized by the Mississippi, not only because of its largeness but because my father showed me on the U.S. map that the Mississippi cut all the way through the country, snaking its way to the Gulf of Mexico. Now this was something big to think about! It held me in its spell!

I had seen the musical *Showboat* and saw a world on the Mississippi that was foreign to me in my small town. It was magic and mystery. (Partly because I earned a dime selling Pepsi bottles, ditched my sister, and sneaked to the movies instead of doing my homework.) And because my father had once had three stitches on his lip and now a small scar, I knew the danger of diving in off its shore and hitting logs on the bottom. Depth and mystery and danger! It was all a young girl needed for a companion to imagine and write.

Flowing water and boats as symbols of change are often used in poetry. An excerpt from my poem, *Gateway*, used the water and a boat like this:

A poem in its existence offers a chance to find self-blessing.
Like a boat waiting in the underbrush,
to be taken out in the sea,
the rune knows its purpose,
and in its being,
all letters and words, is content.

EXERCISES:

✦ Try writing a poem using *rushes* or *sea* or *boat* while talking of your spiritual growth.

✦ How have you been touched by a river?

✦ When you review your life, can you list times you have been fluid and able to flow with what life has given you? Resisted? What was the difference in how your days felt and the outcome?

45. CREATURE OF THE NIGHT (cats)

> "That cat is in love with me, but to say that it's mutual
> doesn't begin to describe anything. I'm totally irrational
> about her. She and I are a scandal."
>
> HELEN GURLEY BROWN

MY SON and his wife, Greg and Wendy, have a stray cat they adopted several years ago. They feel open-hearted and warm when he comes into bed with them and snuggles under the covers. He purrs when sitting on my son's chest and licks Wendy's hand and face. Perhaps he thinks she's one of his own! During the holidays, he stalks the Christmas tree and paws at the ornaments. When he's lucky enough to get an ornament to fall, he treats it as a mouse and bats at it, picks it up and throws it in the air, watches it, pats it again.

Yesterday it was hailing in San Francisco, which is very unusual, and they watched him out the back door as he ran the wrong way, confused, and hid under a thin bush. They coaxed him to come inside, and he dashed through the hail into the house. Duey brings up warm protective feelings they both have, and he teaches them about the cat spirit of good fortune and good company.

Cats are animals that can show great affection. A young friend, Barbara, told me a story of how a cat helped when Barbara was just home from the mental hospital. Her sister's kitty, who was suffering with leukemia, was crying upstairs saying, "Help me. Help me." Even though Barbara wasn't well, she went upstairs to help the tiny thing, and the kitty came to her and chased the snake that was slithering across the floor in Barbara's hallucination. Barbara wondered why a cat would be chasing her hallucination but was grateful for the help.

The cat is so alert and quick to avoid danger that the legend grew that it had nine lives. In addition to this, because a cat can fall from great heights and land on its feet, we say that a person who lands on his feet like a cat means he fares well in difficult situations.

In some places in Cambodia, even today, the cat is associated with drought and rain. They have a custom whereby neighbors place cats in cages and walk door to door in procession through the village praying for rain with song. Water is poured over the cat and its howls are to awaken Indra, the maker of rain. In Ancient China the cat was thought to be a good omen. They also found the cat to be beautiful and graceful; the villagers imitated its gait in dances.

Sacred cats were associated with the sun goddess and an attribute of beauty and love until the Christians, not wanting people to pray to the sun goddess, made cats and what they considered false gods an attribute of witches.

Cats and witchcraft were linked in Pagan religions, and many an old crone had a cat for company and obtained its help in magic. Many an executed witch in the sixteenth century had the company of a cat as she went to her spirit, which is why many independent women the world around praise the cat, a symbol of loyalty and intuition (special knowing).

Cats are among the most common dream animals. They often stand for intuitive feminine wisdom and imagination. In psychological analysis, the cat stands for the powers of the subconscious and what it holds for us.

As we can see symbolically, a cat can be good or bad depending on the context in which it is used. A cat can be predatory and an animal that stalks through the night. The feral cat is a cat who has "gone wild," and although it may live less than half as long as a domestic cat, it is often twice the size and can be frightening. Cats are associated with the moon and the mysteries of the dark. In the West, we associate the black cat with lust and darkness. To have a black cat cross your path is bad luck.

I once had a client who had a negative personal symbol with a cat. To me it showed how personal symbols evolve out of our experiences. As a young child living in an urban renewal area, she was delighted when she saw a cat on the sidewalk and followed it into an abandoned house where a hobo badly frightened her. From that day on, she strongly disliked cats. Later in her life, she used hypnotherapy to help uncover this memory and do some releasing of feelings. The repressed memory came up and, in time, was released. Now she can enjoy cats from a distance and can go to samba class where a cat watches from the desk of the teacher. She also feels better with the understanding of why she has always liked to stay close to home and recently bought tickets to travel to Mexico to see the ancient ruins in the Yucatan.

The cat can been seen as a helper, as Frances Carpenter in her book, *Wonder Tales of Dogs and Cats*, recounts in an ancient story from Japan. It is the story of a boy who draws cats instead of doing his lessons. Even though he tries to be an obedient student and son, he cannot obey the command to not draw cats. His father, at his wit's end, sends him to a temple school where the good priests can surely cure him of drawing cats. They cannot, and in his disappointment with himself, the child runs away. At nightfall he comes to an empty temple and decides to clean the temple hall so if the priests come back they will be pleased and allow him to stay. After sweeping, he decides to draw some cats on the temple walls as he is prone to do. The cats look so fierce and lifelike that the boy frightens himself, and he decides to sleep in a small room on the side of the hall. Upon awakening, he rings the temple bell as he was trained to do. The people of the village come to see who has rung the bell. They find the boy in the small room and together they open the door to the large hall. There had been a terrible fight, and in the center of the room, a giant rat lay dead. It seems the cats flew off the walls and rid the temple of this rat, the same rat who had scared the priests away. From that day on, the boy is a hero, and spends his life as a famous artist drawing cats even for Emperors.

EXERCISES:

+ What does a cat symbolize for you? Can you think of something new after reading this chapter?

+ Do you have negative personal symbols that you can begin to work on? What are they, and how could you ease the way to a change of feelings?

+ What does your feminine knowing tell you of special connections at first meetings?

46. SCOUNDREL OR SAGE *(dogs)*

"Dogs are the most amazing creatures;
they give unconditional love.
For me they are the role model for being alive."

GILDA RADNER

THE DOG is a symbol of loyalty and faithfulness because of its ability to bond with humans when it is separated from its pack. Because the dog retains some human understanding and sympathies, in Native American lore the dog was originally thought to be human. It is these qualities of "humanness" that made the dog "man's best friend."

Evidence from the Celts, however, suggests that it was women who first domesticated dogs. In myth, we know that the goddess who was often known as the "Bitch Goddess" allowed dogs to accompany her when she guarded the gates of the underworld to help both guide the dead and to act as intermediaries between the two worlds. Diana, the huntress, was said to travel with her dogs, and once when Lancelot trespassed on her land, she shot him with her bow and arrow in the buttock to teach him a lesson.

A neighbor's child has a toy fox terrier with big brown eyes; a spot of brown around the left eye; a coat of white short hair; and a short, friendly wagging tail. She got to pick him out from a litter of pups born outside under a large front porch. They were very close, and Fox, as she called him, liked to nestle up to her whenever he could. He was not usually allowed in bed with her, but when she was sick, her mother looked the other way, and Fox would sleep under the covers in the curve of her legs, with his head resting on her knee. What she remembered best was the body warmth and the soft, wet nose that reminded her she was okay and not alone.

Dogs are also used for work functions such as sheepdog, hunter, or guard. The border collie controls sheep with a hypnotic stare that breeders call "eyes." The Celts prized dogs such as boxers, dobermans, and rottweilers for their ability as guard dogs. Other dogs are know for their capacity for hunting, and willingness to help in warfare. Traditionally, dogs help men and are usually thought of as masculine and a sign of male aggression. The dog is a psychological symbol of a balance between man and his inner nature.

Because the dog has a good nose for scenting unseen prey, another psychological symbol for dog can be perception or intuition or the sensing when something is wrong. A trained search and rescue dog can follow scents across the surface of calm water. Signal dogs such as German shepherds and golden retrievers are trained to signal their owners when the phone or doorbell rings, a smoke detector goes off, or even when a baby cries. Dogs remind us how interrelated humans and animals really are and ask us to honor both our spirit and theirs.

After taking recent beach walks with my new friend, Pepper, a fourteen pound female poodle dressed in black curls, it was curious to watch her hunting nature. I had always thought of a poodle as a decorative pet of a dog, but I could clearly see that Pepper had a different self-image. Her hunting instinct was strong, and she hunted everything she could on that coastline sand. And she is one of the first dogs I've seen fly; when her mistress, Pat, comes in the door, her four legs are way, way off the ground!

Naturalist John Muir is quoted as saying in *The Story of My Boyhood and Youth*, "Thus godlike sympathy grows and thrives and spreads far beyond the teaching of churches and schools, where too often the mean, blinding, loveless doctrine is taught that animals have neither mind nor soul, have no rights that we are bound to respect, and were made only for man, to be petted, spoiled, slaughtered, or enslaved." I use this passage from the later half of the nineteenth century because Muir had a growing awareness as he studied and wrote and tramped around in nature. Many of us have come to believe that dogs and all animals are sentient beings just as we are, no more and no less. Living creatures all.

In an ancient story a dog was sacrificed and then brought back to life. The grateful dog wagged its tail, and this is how tail wagging began.

I have learned many lessons from dogs in my life. The golden retriever teaches me loyalty and kindness. I have seen them serve as loyal friends to people with AIDS through the PAW program, which helps the ill adopt dogs for help, company, and caring. For the ill to have a constant, loyal companion is a miracle of love. I have seen shepherds help a blind person cross at the busy intersection of University Avenue and Shattuck in Berkeley, California, with the traffic light signaling "go" to unseeing eyes and a bird call sound signaling "go" to hearing ears. This is an experience of man and nature and technology at its best!

EXERCISES:

+ What experiences have allowed you to feel connected to dogs? How does that connection help you link to your spiritual nature?

+ How have you shown and been shown loyalty? How are you loyal to your spirit and your spiritual path?

+ Write a four-line poem using a dog as part of its sound or image. Here's an example:

Heat and silence in the valley.
In the distance, a dog barks,
memories of trains passing by
or a short walk toward something.

47. THE RED ROUND *(apples)*

"The wild apple trees were one shout of joy."
ANNE BOSWORTH GREENE

THE APPLE has been a sexist symbol in religious writings and rituals since ancient times. The Latin word *malum* means both apple and evil. The image of the forbidden apple that tempts and results in evil is repeated in the Christian Bible and in fairy tales of the poisoned apple (given to good stepchildren by the evil stepmother). The apple was given the meaning of knowledge, both good and evil. We are at a time in our history when feminist women and men can reclaim this round and juicy fruit and give it new symbolic meanings: feminine, round, ripe sexuality and physical desire that is healthy and lusty.

Imagine this: the apple tree in spring with its lovely pinkish-white blossoms. The blossoms are delicate and fall in the breeze like tiny pieces of lace covering the ground. A ground for weddings and rituals of love, a symbol of good luck. The apples ripen in the summer and fill a family's pantry with jellies and sauce. The freezer is filled with apple pies, and children do their first cooking by cutting an apple and adding cinnamon and a bit of water to make baked apple for their lunch. Women who have cooked enough in their lives dispense with cooking and choose organic apples, ripe and round, for their dessert and share this with their friends. The apple of desire is what a woman who has given service all her life chooses to eat for her reward.

When the apples have fallen and been used, the tree continues to bring shade to the yard for the child's play. Grown-ups set up lawn chairs for reading in the protection of the thick limbs and leafy foliage. The tree trunk and limbs gnarl like a sculpture of time.

I once wrote, "I want to die like my friend's apple tree, still giving shade and apples, / just giving out at the bark." We spent many happy hours together reading on her deck under the shade of her apple tree. When I think of her, I think of that tree and the love we share. I think of her living through hard times to create a life she now enjoys that includes leisure time, friendship, reading, conversation, and a favorite tree. Apple, a symbol of giving.

In an essay in *The Alphabet of the Trees* by Christian McEwen, there is a story of trying to teach third graders to write poetry using the sense of touch and being shown a copy of Reinhard Dohl's *Pattern of Poem with an Elusive Intruder*. This is a concrete poem in the shape of an apple. The essayist writes, "Its entire text consists of the word *apfel* repeated over and over, except for the one intruding *wurm*." Of course, kids were drawn away from explaining things by simply drawing their hands or an apple and filling it in with words about the self or the experience.

EXERCISES:

✦ Draw a picture of an apple and fill it with words that seem "to fit."

✦ What new myth or story could you write about the apple to help it find its rightful place in history?

✦ Imagine using a place in nature for your spirit's resting place. Do you know a place you would choose? Can you find one? Describe what it looks like (would look like).

48. A FINGERPRINT OF LAND *(islands)*

> "Islands are gregarious animals,
> they decorate the oceans in convoys."
>
> STELLA BENSON

AN ISLAND can be looked at as a fingerprint of land. A land that is cut off from the major land masses and is individual to itself. Islands evoke sanctuary, a place to be alone and heal oneself. Perhaps the sound of the ocean on every side allows us to hear something new to ease our life.

Looking at islands from a plane's vista, we can see the magic of being set adrift away from the modern day's hustle and bustle. I dreamed about this busyness one night in a hotel room after a flight. In the dream I was flying around on ice skates wearing a long taffeta skirt with a cumbersome bustle. I got the picture!

A poet-scientist friend remembers good times in his childhood wading out to the islands in the Potomac River when the river was low. The channel-bar islands were forested with hardwood trees of willow and cottonwood, the longer islands with oak. Once they got to the islands, he and his father would rock climb, build a fire, and have lunch. The excitement was really in getting and being there.

To survive on an island also seems to be a fantasy of challenge for many of us. The books *Robinson Crusoe* and *Swiss Family Robinson* detail the hardships one would encounter and how to go about making shelter and obtaining food. The recent reality television show *Survivor* used this archetypal fantasy and millions of us watched from our comfortable couches as contestants made shelter and ate bugs and rats.

In dreams, the island is the land of the unknown, the place with a wealth of surprises. It is a special place for perfect dreams where wishes can rest until they are reached in the future. This is what encourages stories of people going off to islands to find themselves. Perhaps our exploration of space is the longing and search for a new "island." Even the fountain of youth is often said to be found on an island.

Because of isolation on islands in the middle of the South Pacific, the Polynesian culture was stable with regard to the environment. Because there was no metal for weapons or clay for bricks, there was no incentive to burn wood for kilns or forges. The island interiors were not suited for farming due to the steep terrain so there was no reason to clear the forests. They did not bring goats or rabbits to the island so the forest was not destroyed by feral animals. The end result was that the forests, soil, watersheds, and water supply were kept in natural harmony, and the people could feed from the coast food supply that depended on clear water.

The only reference I can think of where an island is limited is when psychologist Carl Jung explains the conscious mind versus the unconscious mind. He uses an island as a metaphor for the conscious mind in the sea of the inconceiveable vastness of the subconscious mind where unknown potentials and possibilities live and long for expression.

In an essay in *Seductive Beauty of the Great Salt Lake: Images of a Lake Unknown*, Ella Sorensen writes, "Gunnison Island, nestled deep in the northern arm of Great Salt Lake, is barely 155 acres. It is but a spot on the map. The railroad trestle that split the lake in two—drastically changing the lake's ecology—has, in an odd way, been the salvation of a large pelican colony, for it acts as a buffer against human disturbance." The pelican colony, the largest in North America, breeds on the saddle of the island each year. They sacrifice nearby foraging area on freshwater marshes for the safety from predators that the island nesting site provides. "Parent birds make flights of many miles to freshwater marshes to fish for themselves and their nestlings," says Sorensen, and we learn that islands are indeed places to entrust with our young, and that birds, like human animals, have the will to survive and adapt. Perhaps it also brings to mind that our emphasis should be on growth and that we have time to rechannel the flow of our high-mountain valley that cradles the great salt lake.

In Hindu tradition the island is a magical "elsewhere," a world set apart for gods or those who want some relief from the material world. For Shakespeare, in *The Tempest*, an island is a magical place where wrongs are righted. In a recent workshop I attended, the Buddhist teacher explained detachment not as being an island that is whole to oneself but being the island that is part of all the world: the self joined with the waters and land—becoming everything, thereby finding out what it is to be human.

EXERCISES:

+ What memories do you have of living in harmony with nature? Or of stepping into a scene where nature seemed preserved and in balance? What did those times feel like to you?

+ How can you take refuge from chaos in your life?

+ How could *islands* and *wondering* be associated in your mind? What would you wonder about?

+ Traditionally, there have been many islands just for women. Why do you think this is so, and what would you envision a retreat or life on one of these to be?

49. A PLACE OF SHELTER *(caves)*

> "The dark has to be contained in the light
> or the light will be contained in the dark."
>
> NANCY HALE

THE CAVERN includes cave and grotto and serves as the archetypal meaning of the maternal womb. The archetypal meaning of the cavern is a place in the earth where a passageway may lead you to rebirth or initiation for renewal.

Ancient rituals often had members enter a cave to "return to the womb." In the cave they were bound and had to escape to free their souls from bondage and find spiritual freedom. To enter a cavern and leave was to have the chance to break through to your true nature and new beginnings.

The cave also represented the passageway between the material world to a better, more holy world, so royal marriages were often performed in caves as a symbol of a marriage between heaven and earth, king and queen.

In the Zen Buddhist tradition we must all go to the dragon cave. The dragon is there with a jewel that stands for enlightenment. If we want the jewel, we must journey to our disavowed self. At the Zen retreat Green Gulch, in Bolinas, California, the giant bell is actually a dragon with 500 nipples, signifying the great mother. The great dragon lives in the valley of the retreat. We ring the bell and call the dragon and do the work of spiritual practice.

A photographer friend, Kathryn, finds herself drawn to light coming into caves. She finds these surprising rays of light in even the darkest places, a celebration and an entrée into the mysteries. She told me she was recently out with her camera in a park in Sonoma County where a cabin once stood in which Robert Louis Stevenson had lived for a summer while writing. Near the foundation of his old cabin, she found the entrance to a cave. Never being one to walk away from a challenge, she stepped inside and found a beam coming through the back of the cave that took her breath away. She said she felt as if she were praying.

Later she was told she had entered an old mining shaft and that around the corner, past the light, there are tracks and remains of the work once done inside the earth. She said maybe the power of the miners hardship was part of the power and the prayer.

A client once told me of making caves in the hayloft. If the hay was loose you could dig your way in and hide to your heart's content, with the smell of hay surrounding you. She told me that she would make a cave out of anything she could find: grapevines, weeping willows, foliage, and twisted vines. When she vacationed with her parents, driving from Iowa to New York State, she had the chance to go into a cave that had huge, dark shadows and rocks naturally sculpted into female shapes. She loved the musky smells and echoes and the adventure of actually exploring a muddy cave.

She looked for the hidden in nature and told me of studies that said a high number of writers who suffered the early loss of a parent used nature for healing. My guess is that loss and the love of nature for healing are linked, whether we write or not, because nature is an available source of comfort to all of us at any age in some way.

I know for me nature is a way to pray, and going into the dark helps me find life. Another way of saying this is that entering the area of shadow makes me whole and helps me pass the clouds that are in my way of "spirit seeing."

Caves have helped me ponder my shopping bag filled with life. When my father died, I could feel a part of me went with him: my hopes and dreams and plans we had together. This was not a bad thing, I later realized, any thing we do with our heart can be dangerous. I still had more than enough to live on. But the darkness of the cave allowed me to shed just a little light on the subject until I had enough strength to shed more light on this loss, see it in its totality, and then work through it. Nature gives us herself and allows us stillness and darkness, some growing light.

I wondered how I could send my father to heaven or a spirit place when he was an atheist, and then I remembered, the kind minister at the Cuyahoga

Falls Congregations Church who held the memorial service and funeral for my father even though he used to disturb most sermons with a loud sigh. I realized the cave could hold my father and his darkness and there was spirit in that shadow cave. Nothing needed to be perfect. Nature doesn't demand sense. It is, and it will accept us.

Working with my clients and their dreams, I find that the cave is the place where many go to sort out self from the collective ideas of family and culture. From deep introspection in the cave, the task is to integrate all that they know and find their own beliefs. They absorb ideas and qualities that are correct for them and leave the rest behind. They become their own person. Psychologists call this becoming differentiated.

When I was just entering high school, I took a job in the summer as a day camp leader. One hot summer day I was leading a hike with a group of young girls and boys between eight and ten years old. We found a cave made by rock slides at the side of a high hill. It wasn't easy to discover the opening, because rocks were grouped around the mouth of the cave and made an opening the size of a small window. I slipped through the "window" and after slowly feeling my way down a long passageway found a large cave with a bit of light coming through at one side.

The children called this "their secret house" and were very serious in noting the path and the rock formations and trees surrounding the cave to help them recognize the way back for next week's hike. We brought flashlights back with us and went inside together discovering little rocklike rooms at the back of the cool cave where we could lie down or group together. The girls had one ledge and the boys the other. Every week, they smuggled in rations: towels, water, cookies, comic books, extra batteries. Different kids were responsible for stories to tell, and I told ghost stories and gave them corn chips and grape juice. I was the most popular counselor at that camp on Wednesdays! I was young and looked eagerly forward to it myself!

We had no mishap, and it's a wonderful memory of exploration and excitement, a time when we built a cavern home to play and dream in. However, even at fifteen, I realized that it could be dangerous in its hiding and darkness. Instead of danger, however, the feminine symbol of the heart of home gave us a place to reflect and be with our spirited excitement.

EXERCISES:

+ When have you gone into the dark to understand yourself as different from others?

+ What does the image of a cave bring up for you? What could be a symbol for you?

+ Write about this. Mystery and the dreams of hidden things: damp basements, animals lost and found in the dark, letters hidden in pockets whispering, *Come to the tunnel, come to the cave.*

50. HEART OF THE WORLD *(turquoise)*

"Turquoise, my lover's eye, mate to the sky."

DONNA MCGUINN

THE GEMSTONE turquoise is a mineral deposit valued for its beautiful blue-green color. It is found mainly in Persia. Turkish traders thought it a beautiful stone and believed it brought luck; hence, its name refers back to Turkey. The Turkish traders brought it into Europe to the delight of many Westerners.

Turquoise was used as currency in many Native American tribes. In Western traditions, turquoise is the birthstone of those born under the sign of Sagittarius, and lovely jewelry is made in recognition of their date of birth. In the sixties, turquoise jewelry was part of the "hippie" fashion of the day and a symbol of Jupiter (green pigment) or Venus (blue pigment).

Maria Leach writes in *Folklore, Mythology and Legend* that "Turquoise is to the Tibetans what jade is to the Chinese. They believe it to be a stone of good fortune, physical well-being, and a protection against contagion and evil eye, a belief that is quite general. Hindu mystics say it will bring immeasurable wealth if on first looking at the new moon, you immediately look at a turquoise. It is the national stone of Persia, and Iranian peasants place a piece of turquoise in a sheep's eye as an amulet against the evil eyes. In Northern India it is worn in the water to protect a bather from serpents and boils."

She goes on to say about Turquoise Woman, a Navaho Indian deity, "In some accounts she is a variant of Changing Woman, chief female deity of the Navaho. In other accounts she is said to have been created, together with White Shell Woman, by Changing Woman's epidermis rubbed from under Changing Woman's breasts."

Hans Biedermann tells us in his *Dictionary of Symbolism* that "In ancient Mexico, also, the turquoise (in Aztec, xihuitl) was one of the most admired gemstones; only jade was more valued. Turquoise mosaics adorned the diadem of the kings and their ornamental shields. The fire god was called "Lord of the Turquoise" (Xiuhtechuli)—the sky-blue turquoise symbolizing the unity of heavenly (i.e., solar) and earth fire. He was adorned with the "turquoise serpent" (Xiuhcoat) which also constituted his 'alter ego'; the Aztec king was considered to be his earthly counterpart."

In the myth from ancient Central America, when the warrior-god, the Sun, woke, he would drive the Moon and the stars from the sky armed with the "turquoise serpent," identified with fire and the Sun's rays.

"The cult-room of the Pueblo Indian high-priest of the Rains (Lord of the Northern Rains), so closely guarded a secret that it is practically never revealed to a European, contains an altar comprising 'two small crystal and turquoise columns and a heart-shaped stone, the heart of the world," write Chevalier and Gheerbrant in *Dictionary of Symbols.*

EXERCISES:

+ What is at the heart of your world? Consider building an altar there.

+ Go to a rock shop or jewelry store and look for pieces of turquoise. Study a piece carefully and see what message it has for you.

+ A pictograph is a story told in pictures. We know that from early times cave dwellers drew with charcoal-burnt sticks on the walls of their caves. Thinking of the myth of the turquoise God chasing the sun out of the sky each day to make night, draw this. Now think of myths that you live by and draw some. (For example, I used to think a boss was very important in my life and I felt intimidated. Also, a myth I now live by is that imagination is a great healer.)

51. LOCKS OF HAIR *(hair)*

"The seated woman has closed her eyes.
Her head gradually tilted
toward the haul of the brush.
She is lulled by rhythm and the sweet tug
at her scalp, along the nape of her neck, down
the left shoulder. She feels the brush,
the hand guiding it and she leans
toward the other who takes her time."

C. B. FOLLETT

TOUCHING and combing another person's hair can be a very intimate act. Of course, lovers often show caring by combing the hair of the loved one. It can be very soothing and relaxing, which is probably why there is an old Russian custom whereby the students do not comb their hair the night before exams so they do not lose concentration.

Carrying someone's hair in a locket shows a strong connection for a loved one and was a widely practiced custom in the nineteenth century. A lock of hair was thought to contain part of the person's soul and was a vow between lovers. In folklore, the sea fairy often made magic as she combed her own hair. However, gypsies believed a lock of another person's hair gave you power over the soul of the person, and they would use locks of hair in spells.

Hair continues to grow briefly after death, symbolizing life force and strength. Hair has been used as the symbol for the growing consciousness of a person, and when it is cut, it represents a threat to the course of a person's development. In the Old Testament, Delilah cut Samson's hair, causing him to lose his strength.

In the story of Rapunzel, a prince's passageway to love is when the princess lets down her hair and entreats him to climb up to a high window to save her. In a Spanish-American folktale, a girl is buried alive and her hair is filled with sorrow and grows through the ground into a bush. The wind hears the bush's sad song and saves the girl from her unjust death.

Hair can be a literal protection in the world of animals too. The world's largest and most powerful hunter, the polar bear, has dense fur that keeps it warm even when temperatures drop to forty below zero Celsius. "An undercoat of thick fur is protected by an outer coat of long guard hairs. These hairs stick together when wet, forming a waterproof barrier. Under the fur, a thick layer of blubber performs two roles, insulating the bear against the cold and acting as a food store to help the bear survive hard times," writes Miranda Smith in *Living Earth*. She continues, "The thick coats of the mountain apes, that live in the mountain forest of the Virunga volcanoes in Africa keep out the chill, while water runs off the outer layers of hairs." Moreover, even as the body hair protects the aduts, so does it keep the babies warm and dry as the mother wraps her shaggy arms around them.

Barbara G. Walker informs us in *The Woman's Encyclopedia of Myths and Secrets* that "the ancients insisted that women needed their hair to work magic spells; thus women deprived of their hair were harmless. For this reason, Christian nuns and Jewish wives were compelled to shave their head. Inquisitors of the medieval church insisted on shaving the hair of accused witches before putting them to the torture."

However women were not to shave their own head. If a woman cut her own hair, it was showing a lack of conformity, a sign of rebellion. Cutting off her hair was one of the crimes for which Joan of Arc was condemned to the fire.

Today independent woman do as they please and use their hair as a sign of allegiance to themselves. The famous Mexican painter, Frida Kahlo, shaved her head as a sign of her grief and didn't care what anyone thought of it when she found out that her husband, Diego Rivera, was unfaithful .

As we write we keep a record of our humanness: grief, rebellion, joy. We write to remember we are alive with all that matters and to honor our feelings and spiritual connections to the mother changing and moving beneath our footsteps. Often we write to find out how we feel, and this longing in itself helps us grow. Sometimes it helps to write about our physical being: our hair, our femininity, our beauty.

There are many beliefs and traditions surrounding the cutting of hair. A child's hair was often not cut until the toddler years were over as a way of strengthening his or her constitution. Today a child's hair is often not cut to symbolize a few years of freedom from gender roles.

Monks heads are shaved to symbolize their commitment to the church and their renouncement of the liberties of the ordinary person. Head shaving was their initiation to allow the subconscious energies to become more alive as they retreated from the everyday world and returned to the hairless state of the newborn.

Most women would agree that we have been taught that our hair and our hairdo is very important to our beauty. "The three most important things to a Southern girl are God, family, and hair, almost never in that order," writes Lucinda Ebersole in *The New York Times Magazine*. It often symbolizes our place in society, which is shown by Marge Piercy's writing in *Braided Lives*, "[Long hair] is considered bohemian, which may be why I grew it, but I keep it long because I love the way it feels, part cloak, part fan, part mane, part security blanket."

Hair fashions often represent different decades. An up-to-date hairdo is a sign of a person who is modern and keeps up with her time. I remember my grandmother pulling back her long hair and rolling a dark stocking into her bun to make it look fuller, as was the style of the day. Then came the bob, the bouffant, the page boy, the pixie, the mohawk, until today we have the young with jagged cuts and shaven heads. Each decade a new generation of youth makes statements of what it is to be young in their time and place by the style of their hairdo. It's important for us to honor their attempt to separate and speak for themselves, for only they know what it is like to mature into what we have built for them.

EXERCISES:

+ Hair has often been a sign of power for women. Write about your own personal power.

+ The shaving of a head can be surrender or punishment, a vow, a fashion. Write about each one and what resonates to you spiritually.
+ Thinking about Joan of Arc, write about anger and the important place anger has on our spiritual path.

+ Writing can help release body memories so we can find forgiveness for others for the wrongdoing done to our sisters. Write a prayer to a sister of yesteryear.

52. THE LOVED ONES *(beetles)*

A priest asked with Dr. J. B. Haldane,
the famous scientist, what he could say
about our creator from the study of his works.
Dr. Haldane replied, "An inordinate fondness of beetles."

THERE ARE MORE species of beetles than any other insect in the world. This is nature in its abundance ,with the busy beetles on the forest floor giving help in recycling. Kick a rotting log and you may have find hundreds of beetles inside eating the dead wood.

When I was "birding" recently on a pickleweed marsh in Sonoma County, a girl of about eight let me look in her bug jar to see a small, striped insect. She explained to me that it was a ladybug but not with spots and that they were in the nearby woods hibernating in large masses. She told me they were helpful to us by eating aphids. I told her the one fact I knew, that ladybugs were once called lady birds and were considered lucky in England; this was because they believed Mary, the mother of their Christian God, loved the lady birds best of all insects. She seemed satisfied with my knowledge, and I was amazed at hers.

In the winter I would see hundreds of these little beetles clinging together under bark or to the sides of large boulders in the redwood parklands. A park ranger told me that just as we seek shelter and bundle together against the wind so do these little creatures. She also told me that the nursery rhyme, "fly away home / your house is on fire, / your children do roam" came from the widespread practice in Europe of burning vines of the grape harvest where ladybugs had laid their eggs.

THE WISE EARTH SPEAKS

In South America insects were seen as souls of the dead revisiting earth. Some ancients thought they were messengers from a star. It might be helpful to mine these meanings in your writings and wonder who might be visiting you and for what spiritual purpose. Or, what the stars might want to tell you.

I remember our family sitting on the front stoop of our house when the sun had gone down but it was too hot and humid to sleep. We'd drink iced tea and small talk watching the stars and the fireflies. (My young brother would get a glass jar and we'd poke holes in the top and allow firefly capture awhile in the interest of scientific inspection.)

A firefly is actually a "beetle with the uncanny ability to produce light. They use their luminous organs to send coded messages in darkness, all in the interest of reproduction. The male . . . flashes a message to indicate his interest in a mate. Seeing it, a female of his kind responds with her light. The male makes a quick U-turn and flashes again, and the female replies. He comes in for a landing on the leaf where she rests," writes author Les Lines in *The Audubon Society Book of Insects*. Fireflies are a lovely reminder that there is a vast beauty earth offers, the whole of it offered in pieces tiny enough to hold.

One beetle, the earwig, named for its habit of flying into human ears, was made into medicine to cure earaches. Sometimes today the beetle is a metaphor for someone who works too hard, because of their industry and brittle shell seemingly acquired by long hours of work.

After watching a documentary show on television about the Australian Aboriginals, who call the spiritual and everyday life, the Dreaming, or Dreamtime, I dreamed I lay on my stomach in a hot, open field watching beetles try to fly. It was a vulnerable feeling to be there alone and watching this effort. They seemed to try and try, on and on. Finally one got its wings wide enough open, and off it went. Some did manage. I woke up feeling wrung out with effort. I felt it was a story showing that I didn't need to try so hard. Personal symbols, a chance to rethink behaviors in the vein of a spiritual life.

The Dreamtime helps remind me that writing often leads the way for our consciousness. Writing is like the tall grass in the green meadow, springing up from the depths of soil and earth, coaxing us to write what we will come to know. As we write, our truth lies before us, a message for our spiritual path, and we become more of ourselves, the selves that live in us, around us, and in relationship to other people.

The word for "scarab beetle" in Egyptian means "The Becoming One," denoting the beetle as a symbol of creation. Also, like the force that could move the sun across the sky, the beetle could roll its egg by itself. Because of this the beetle became a symbol of dawn and creation. The color blue of the scarab also aligned it to the sky and its heavens.

Alison Jones's *Dictionary of World Folklore* tells us that the scarab, "one of the most famous of ancient amulets, was worn by the living to protect themselves from death and by the dead to ensure the restoration of their vital heat in the next world." The scarab beetle was carried by the living for good luck because the beetle lays but one egg at a time, showing the importance of life. Scarabs became a fad in the 1960s with the hippies and lovers of the earth as a symbol of connection to the earth and good life fortune. Scarab amulets were once buried with one's beloved to help create good passage and happy eternal life.

Other beliefs about scarabs include the one from Africa where natives of the Congo thought the scarab to be a symbol of the sun and of eternal reward. The Egyptians thought that the scarab symbolized fertility in males. South American tribes believed there was a Great Beetle who was the creator.

EXERCISES:

+ Do you believe in the reincarnation of sentient beings? If so, how does that belief affect your life? If not, how is your life affected?

+ How are you the "becoming one"?

BIBLIOGRAPHY

Biedermann, Hans, *Dictionary of Symbolism: Cultural Icons and the Meanings Behind Them*, Meridian: Penguin Books, New York, NY 1994. The power of symbols and their origins.

Bruce-Mitford, Miranda, *The Illustrated Book of Signs and Symbols*, KK Publishers, New York, NY 1996. Illustrations and description of signs and symbols.

Busch, Phyllis, *Wildflowers*, Charles Scribner's Sons, New York, NY 1977. The stories behind the names.

Carroll, David M., *Trout Reflections*, St. Martin's Press, New York, NY 1993. A poetic fisherman's tales of fishing.

Chetwynd, Tom, *A Dictionary of Symbols*, Paladin Grafton Books, London, England 1982. Guide to the language of symbols.

Chevalier, Jean and Gheerbrant, Alain, *The Dictionary of Symbols*, Penguin Books, London, England 1969. A rich inventory of symbols.

Cooper, J. C., *An Illustrated Encyclopaedia of Traditional Symbols*, Thames and Hudson Ltd., London, England 1978. Symbols to open up levels of understanding.

Dunning, Joan, *Secrets of the Nest*, Houghton Mifflin Co., New York, NY 1994. Variety of birds, nests, and egg stories with lovely illustrations.

Follett, C. B., *Beside the Sleeping Maiden*, Arctos Press, Sausalito, CA 1999. Poems of the earth by Marin County poets.

Fontana, David, *The Secret Language of Dreams*, Chronicle Books, San Francisco, CA 1994. A visual key to dreams and their meanings.

Fontana, David, *The Secret Language of Symbol*, Chronicle Books, San Francisco, CA 1993. Visual key to symbols and their meanings.

Emerson, Dr. William K. and Old, William E., *Seashells of North America*, Golden Press, New York, NY 1968.

Golomb, Elan, *Trapped in the Mirror*, William Morrow, New York, NY 1992. Journey back to the self.

Gordis, Daniel, *God Was Not in the Fire: The Search For A Spiritual Judaism*, Scribner, New York, NY 1995. The spiritual in Judaism.

Hogan, Linda, *Dwellings*, W.W. Norton, New York, NY 1995.